Richard Wagner

Titles in the series Critical Lives present the work of leading cultural figures of the modern period. Each book explores the life of the artist, writer, philosopher or architect in question and relates it to their major works.

In the same series

Richard Wagner

Raymond Furness

REAKTION BOOKS

Published by Reaktion Books Ltd
33 Great Sutton Street
London EC1V ODX, UK

www.reaktionbooks.co.uk

First published 2013

Printed and bound in Great Britain
by Bell & Bain, Glasgow

A catalogue record for this book is available from the British Library.
ISBN 978 1 78023 182 2

Contents

Rogelio Egusquiza, *Richard Wagner*, *c*. 1882, etching, aquatint and drypoint.

Introduction

It is more than probable that one should regard him as the greatest
genius that the theatre has ever known.

Egon Friedell

To write succinctly and objectively on Richard Wagner, arguably
the most controversial figure in the entire history of Western
culture and, in the distinguished musicologist Deryck Cooke's
words, 'one of the greatest minds the world has ever known', is
no mean task, for Wagner is a musician unlike any other in his
all-consuming desire to impose upon the world his vision of
what art and life should be.[1] He may be called the supreme
pantopragmatist: Brahms correctly described him as 'a man with
a gigantic capacity for work, colossal industry and horrendous
energy'.[2] His vast collection of writings on a huge variety of topics
fills sixteen substantial volumes and his letters, some 10,000 of
them and many of considerable length, provide many fascinating
insights into his way of thinking. As a musician he was regarded
by Mahler as second only to Beethoven, but he always considered
himself more than a musician: he was also a dramatist and poet (and
it has been suggested that he was 'arguably the greatest European
dramatist since the seventeenth century'[3]), an intellectual writing
on art and society, on the need for myth, on the place of theatre in
the modern world, on politics, on religion, on love and sexuality,
on regeneration. He entered the debate on Jewishness with his

characteristic pugnacity, putting forward views of considerable originality. He remains a unique phenomenon, the only musician to have given his name to a nineteenth-century movement, and was determined to confront the world with his immense achievements in the theatre and with his intellectual concepts: the world must take heed of what he had to teach it. And it was not slow to react.

Dieter Borchmeyer neatly sums up the situation: 'Just as he [Wagner] wanted to have his say on everything, so the whole world now demands to have its say in turn.'[4] Reactions vary from the hagiographical to the most vituperative: he was either (almost) 'God himself' or 'the last little toadstool on the dunghill of Romanticism'.[5] His multifaceted genius brought forth a cascade of responses, a tohu-bohu which frequently seemed more appropriate to the madhouse than to the seminar room, the concert hall or the music academy. Because he cannot be grasped from one single perspective alone he must necessarily encourage a plethora of responses which make him truly unique in musical history. The number of books and articles written on him, it was claimed, had reached the 10,000 mark before his death, overtaking those about any other human being except Jesus of Nazareth and Napoleon.[6] More recent scholarship has been more precise, informing us that shortly after Wagner's death in 1883 more had in fact been written on Shakespeare but up to 1955 'more books had been written on Wagner than about Bach, Beethoven, Mozart, Marx, Schiller or Dickens. Wagner trails Goethe by a short margin, however, and Shakespeare by a consistently larger one.'[7] Still, the need among academics, musicologists, philosophers, historians, theologians, theatre directors, *littérateurs* and sundry scholars (and cranks) to react to Wagner as a cultural phenomenon has rarely abated; Wagner is indelibly *there*, a forbidding and fascinating monument on the cultural landscape of the last century and a half, one of those who have invaded vast territories of the world's mind, the ruthless despot who, it is claimed, boasted that his baton would be the sceptre of the future, teaching the times to come the path they must take.[8]

Eduard Hanslick, mercilessly lampooned, as we shall see, as Beckmesser in *Die Meistersinger von Nürnberg*, suggested mischievously that the Holy Ghost, should it descend again as a dove above the twelve apostles in the modern era, would pose the inevitable question: 'Well, gentlemen, what do *you* think of Richard Wagner?'[9] (Karl Marx, in a letter to his daughter Jenny at the end of August 1876, reports that he had been tormented by this same question.) The tidal wave of responses reached tsunami-like dimensions with approbation battling victoriously against abuse, with parody and persiflage galore. Wagner's influence on, or necessary appearance in, European works of fiction is a study in itself, taking in major literary figures; as a musician he came to represent the apogee of Romanticism, drawing on the work of earlier composers and creating a musical language of overwhelming intensity.[10] It has been persuasively argued that there is no great artist who has travelled so far, pushing early nineteenth-century music to the very boundaries of atonality, developing the orchestra of his day to a 'vast sonorous instrument of unparalleled power and flexibility'.[11] And as a genius with the deepest theatrical instincts he bequeathed the world vast *Gesamtkunstwerke* that exemplified the fusion of the poetic and the musical, creating striking situations which amaze by their expression of feeling, excitement, awe and exaltation.

The Wagner fever reached its climax in the years preceding the First World War, but at the turn of the century dissenting voices began to be heard who objected to the hegemony of German music, and that of Wagner above all. As early as 1905 Debussy, who had earlier acknowledged the genius of Wagner, particularly in *Parsifal*, objected to what seemed to be Wagner's unwholesome influence, describing him as a man whose music was a dangerous opiate; Wagner was also seen as ruthlessly pulling music like a refractory

mare behind him in his egotistical thirst for glory.[12] Erik Satie, witty
and ironic, lampooned the German composer by setting Gothic
pointed arches to music (*Ogives*, 1886). The American Charles Ives,
who had previously admired much of Wagner, later looked back on
his Tristanesque Second Symphony and rejected it all as stuff and
nonsense.[13] It was Stravinsky however, declaring 'I am the present',
who came out most strongly against the whole idea of the *Gesamtkunstwerk* for its lack of tradition and self-importance; his visit to
the Bayreuth Festival of Wagner's music in 1912 had not impressed
him and he welcomed the advent of clarity and rhythmical energy
in music. Béla Bartók also objected to Wagner, arguing that he
was not a source of inspiration and that Liszt was a more fruitful
influence.[14] The war-cry was now '*A bas Wagner!*' ('Down with
Wagner!' – Darius Milhaud). Bayreuth closed its doors from 1914
to 1924; the 1920s, with their *Neue Sachlichkeit* (New Realism) and
Verfremdungseffekte (alienation effects), had little patience with the
theatre of illusion and mythical archetypes, inundated by overwhelming music, and when Ernst Křenek's *Jonny spielt auf* was
all the rage it seemed that Wagner had had his day.

It was then his misfortune to be deified by a psychopath whose
monstrous regime may have, for some, tainted his music for ever.
Wagner's son Siegfried forbad the singing of 'Deutschland über
alles' after the triumphant panegyric to German art (not politics)
at the end of *Die Meistersinger* had been greeted as the national
anthem from a standing audience giving the Nazi salute; after
1933 his Welsh-Danish wife Winifred skilfully encouraged Hitler's
demented Wagner enthusiasm to keep the Bayreuth Festival
solvent. After the collapse of Germany in 1945, the bombing
of Wagner's home, Villa Wahnfried, and the desecration of the
Festival Theatre by 'Anything Goes' and other entertainments for
American troops it did seem that Wagner's rule was finally at an
end, but his rehabilitation was remarkably swift. In 1945 an article
by one R.W.S. Mendel in *Musical Opinion* argued that it would

'Richard Wagner. Höher geht's nimmer' ('Can't get any higher'), a 1913 caricature by Olaf Gulbrannson.

indeed be perverse to share the Nazi view that Wagner had been 'one of theirs'. He had never been: despite the exceptionally high profile he had enjoyed in Nazi propaganda Wagner had actually suffered a steady decline in popularity in German opera houses. In the 1932–3 season he came third in the list of most popular opera composers, after Bizet and Weber; in the 1938–9 season he came twelfth (with *Lohengrin*); in the 1939–40 season he was ousted by Verdi.[15] In Bayreuth the number of performances dwindled rapidly due to the inevitable financial and human costs of the war: between 1940 and 1942 only *Ring* cycles and *Der fliegende Holländer* were given, and from 1943 to 1944 only *Die Meistersinger von Nürnberg* was given for exhausted soldiers from the front whose appreciation may have been somewhat muted. It was also becoming apparent that themes such as redemption, orgasmic extinction, pity and mystical transcendence were becoming increasingly remote from a nation stunned and battered from all sides, with the Führer himself increasingly drawn to Franz Lehár. He also, apparently, liked to hear during his last days records of the music of *Untermenschen* such as Rachmaninov, Tchaikovsky and Borodin, concertos played by the Jewish violinist Bronisław Huberman, founder of the Palestine orchestra (1936), and the Jewish pianist Artur Schnabel.[16]

In 1951 the new Bayreuth opened with a performance of Beethoven's Ninth Symphony conducted by Wilhelm Furtwängler, eight *Ring* cycles, six performances of *Parsifal* (which had not been performed there for twelve years) and seven of *Die Meistersinger*, the baton shared between Herbert von Karajan and Hans Knappertsbusch. The new house now quoted Wagner's own words from *Die Kunst und die Revolution* (Art and Revolution), which insisted that whereas the Greek world of art expressed the spirit of a glorious nation, the art world of the future should express the spirit of a free people regardless of all national boundaries, the national element being no more than an added embellishment, not a constricting limitation. His grandsons Wieland and Wolfgang insisted on a *tabula rasa*, and a new era began.

This study will recount the saga of Wagner's tempestuous life and discuss the operas and music dramas chronologically. His writings, particularly the *Reformschriften* and the essays of his later years, will play an important part; I shall quote from Borchmeyer's handy *Richard Wagner. Dichtungen und Schriften* in ten volumes (Frankfurt am Main, 1983), and volume and page numbers will be given in brackets. Most translations will be my own, but I shall also use English translations from other sources where they are readily available (*My Life*, for example). The secondary literature is, we know, immense and I have necessarily been drastically selective. Our study of this most critical life will end with a brief survey of recent Bayreuth productions and put forward a necessarily tentative and subjective suggestion on how Wagner might ideally be staged in future.

1

The Beginnings

We are still waiting for the man who can compose and write
a genuine opera.

Jean Paul, 27 April 1813, Bayreuth

Daydreaming in the forest, Siegfried, in Wagner's music drama,
wonders what his father might have looked like; it is tempting,
indeed, to interpret this in the light of Wagner's own uncertainty
about his parentage and the number of orphans and half-orphans
in his work. When he commented on 26 December 1878 on the
resemblance between their son Siegfried and 'Father Geyer',
Wagner's stepfather, his wife Cosima made the remark: 'Father
Geyer was certainly your father?' to which Wagner replied: 'I do
not think so.' 'And the resemblance?' Cosima persisted. 'My mother
loved him at that time. It was an elective affinity', Wagner replied.[1]
Did he know the facts himself, hinting evasively at Goethe's problematic novel *Die Wahlverwandtschaften*? (In this book of 1809 the
child born to a married couple resembles neither parent but rather
the agents of those extramarital *amours* about whom both man and
wife were thinking at the moment of the child's begetting.) The
records show that our composer was born in Leipzig on 22 May
1813, son of Johanna Rosine Wagner née Pätz and Carl Friedrich
Wagner, lawyer and police actuary, an amateur actor and according
to E.T.A. Hoffmann 'a somewhat exotic individual'. Two of Wagner's
sisters would become actresses (Rosalie, his favourite, would become

The interior of the 16th-century Lutheran St-Thomaskirche in Leipzig, where Wagner was baptized in 1813.

the first to play Gretchen in Leipzig's production of Goethe's *Faust*); another sister would become a professional singer, as would his brother Albert. Small wonder, then, that the boy's first memories would be of costume, greasepaint and stage sets. When he was two months old his mother took him to Teplitz (now Teplice, Czech Republic), where Ludwig Geyer, a painter, actor, poet and friend of the family, was appearing on the stage. Although the Battle of the Nations had not yet been fought, the country around Leipzig was full of marauding soldiers and it took courage for a woman to undertake the journey with an infant. In August Wagner was christened in St Thomas's Church, Leipzig, a building hallowed and made famous by the music of Johann Sebastian Bach. The hostilities, when they finally broke out in mid-October 1813, brought bombardment and massive slaughter as the armies of the emperors of Russia and Austria fought against the French; the resulting epidemic of typhus caused by the unburied corpses of men and horses claimed the life of Wagner's father.

On 18 August Ludwig Geyer married Wagner's widowed mother and the family moved to Dresden, where Geyer, whose play *Der bethlehemische Kindermord* (The Slaughter of the Innocents) had proved a success and who had been recognized by Goethe himself, was now a member of the Royal Saxon Court Theatre. Two years after this, Carl Maria von Weber was appointed opera director in Dresden and frequently consorted with Geyer and his family (did he, one wonders, see a *tableau vivant* in which young Richard, scarcely five, made his first appearance on the stage as an angel wearing a leotard with wings strapped on his back?). Weber's music would later come as revelation to the adolescent who exulted in the evocation of dark forests and supernatural forces, especially in *Der Freischütz* (The Free-shooter); as a seven-year-old he had played the enchanting 'Bridesmaid Chorus' of Act Three to his dying stepfather. Much later he would play a decisive part in the return of Weber's mortal remains from London, composing a funeral oration in words and music. (The duality between good and evil in *Der Freischütz*, mirrored in the orchestra by a conflict between the keys of C major – light, joy and sanity – and C minor – conflict, defiance and threat – together with the massive chord of C major towards the end of the overture, expressing Agathe's redemptive presence and triumph over the power of Samiel, taught Wagner much, but there would be other mentors, as we shall see).

A war child, then? Born on the eve of a great battle which would check Napoleon's megalomania; carried off, not through whinnying horses and cannonades but through military skirmishes and confusion, to a man who, it is said, was his father; losing his official father some six months later, then brought up as the son of Ludwig Geyer. (In the light of Wagner's later and problematic anti-Semitism there will be much speculation on whether or not Geyer was Jewish: there is no evidence that he was.) Geyer was certainly the surname that the boy would keep throughout his school years, during which he was exposed to the delights of the theatre and surrounded by actors, actresses and singers. Of great importance were the days he spent in Leipzig with his uncle Adolf, a private scholar and eccentric whose library contained much fascinating material. Adolf Wagner had known both Tieck and Hoffmann, corresponded with the novelist Jean Paul and even met Schiller in his youth. When walking through the streets of Leipzig with his nephew in 1828, he would recite whole passages of Shakespeare in German. This nephew, now a pupil at the Nikolai-Gymnasium and fifteen years old, was determined to emulate the British dramatist and write his own play. He was also, it seems, taking lessons in harmony from a member of the Gewandhaus Orchestra: as Beethoven had provided musical accompaniment to Goethe's play *Egmont*, so he, Richard Wagner, was determined to achieve fame as a dramatist first and foremost, while also providing incidental music. *Leubald* was the result (no music is extant). On sending a copy to his uncle, the boy explained that he did not wish any school pedantry to hamper his development. Adolf was not impressed.

The work is a tangled and wild conflation of at least five Shakespeare plays, most obviously *Romeo and Juliet* and *Macbeth*. The hero, Leubald, plans wholescale revenge on Roderick and his house for the murder of Leubald's father Siegmar. Roderick, his sons and all their male relatives are murdered; only Roderick's daughter Adelaide remains, saved by a suitor whom she hated. Leubald murders him and his relations and repairs to the castle of the robber knight who has abducted Adelaide. Leubald is taken prisoner and meets Adelaide in a dungeon; he falls in love with her but realizes that they should be deadly enemies. His father's ghost appears, as do the ghosts of Adelaide's family. To lay the ghosts

Leubald seeks help from a sorceress named Flaming, who seeks to call up from the earth one of the spirits of *Macbeth*. She fails, and the demented Leubald dispatches her. With her dying breath she calls up an army of ghosts and demons; Leubald's reason finally gives way and he stabs Adelaide, then lays his head in her blood-stained lap and expires. Adelaide's faithful maid Gundchen dies at her feet; Astolf, Adelaide's official bridegroom, delivers an oration on one whose mind was deranged and brought to madness.[2]

A farrago of youthful nonsense? In an autobiographical sketch he wrote when he was 30, Wagner tells us that there were 43 corpses in all and that he was obliged to bring back some of them as ghosts to finish the play; he either exaggerated deliberately or forgot that Leubald only killed eight people on the stage and that there were only eighteen dead bodies in all. And to claim that there were 43 bodies out of a cast of 30 does seem rather implausible. It would of course be easy to consign this tale of vengeance, witchcraft, chivalry, murder and Gothic horror to oblivion, but there are premonitions here of *Tristan und Isolde*: a wounded man, dying, transfigured, with the woman he loves and who also dies, close to her devoted maid, and the noble forgiveness of one who had been usurped coming too late.

We see here a budding dramatist, his head full of Shakespeare (in the Schlegel-Tieck translation), and also Goethe: *Götz von Berlichingen* finds undeniable echoes in *Leubald*'s opening tavern scene. But Leipzig was (and still is) a vibrant musical centre and the Gewandhaus concerts, of Beethoven above all, stimulated the young man's sense of drama just as much as the theatre did: Wagner's determination to become a composer dates roughly from this time. And in 1829, when he was just short of his sixteenth birthday, came that overwhelming experience, described in *My Life*, of seeing the singer Wilhelmine Schröder-Devrient as Leonora in Beethoven's *Fidelio*, *the* pivotal moment, he would claim, of his adolescence.[3] The young hot-head delivered a rhapsodic letter to her room at the theatre and then rushed, raving, out into the night. It was with music that he would conquer the world, and Wilhelmine had showed him the way. (She even, we are told, remembered the letter's contents and recited them word for word in 1842 when Wagner was visiting Dresden to audition for *Rienzi*.) A nice anecdote, though modern scholarship has pointed out that there was no performance of *Fidelio* in Leipzig that year, but that Schröder-Devrient did appear as Romeo in Bellini's *I Capuletti e i Montecchi*, which impressed itself on Wagner's imagination.[4] When writing *My Life* 50 years later, Wagner either genuinely confused the two operas or deliberately insisted that it was Beethoven in order to imply that he was Beethoven's natural successor. Wagner always defended Wilhelmine and attacked those who claimed that she 'did not have a voice'; the essay 'Über Schauspieler und Sänger' (On Actors and Singers, 1872) defended her stoutly against critics who argued that she always preferred parlando to singing: she was a great tragedienne, acted gloriously and should not be compared to the 'female castrati' of the time (IX, p. 253). To return to Beethoven: Wagner's growing obsession with the composer would later be seen in the Paris years in his novella *Eine Pilgerfahrt zu Beethoven* (A Pilgrimage to Beethoven) wherein an impoverished German composer, one 'R' from the city of 'L', is taken into Beethoven's confidence while a hapless upper-class English dilettante is cursorily dismissed. Beethoven tells 'R' of the need he felt to incorporate words into the last movement of his Ninth Symphony, and to synthesize words and music in a new art form where arias, duets and other divisions are to be overcome in the continuous fabric of music drama. 'R' listens attentively.[5]

Writing in *The Listener* on 16 May 1963, Harold Truscott explained in his article on the young Wagner that the composer differed from such musical geniuses as Bach, Beethoven, Mozart and Schubert in that the direction of his talent was not clearly defined in early life, being, as it were, a blank cheque to be filled in later. Being surrounded by the theatrical careers of his family, the theatre could indeed have been his métier (and to a certain extent, of course, it always would be), but music, Romantic music and Beethoven above all showed him the path he had to take. And Geyer's personal contact with Weber gave fruitful musical stimuli to the young Wagner. We have mentioned the dark Romanticism of *Der Freischütz*, but there was also Heinrich Marschner, whose opera *Der Vampyr* was first performed in Leipzig in 1828. Marschner was probably the most important exponent of German Romantic opera after Weber; *his* vampire opera, a typical example of *Schauer-romantik* (Romanticism of Horror), was a resounding success and similar in outline to *Der Freischütz*, although transposed to a gloomy Scotland. In it, Lord Ruthven of Marsden sucks the blood of two virgin brides but is prevented from draining the blood of the heroine Malwina and is dragged down to hell amid fiendish laughter. (Scottish settings were popular after Sir Walter Scott; one thinks of *Lucia di Lammermoor* and, of course, the original setting of Wagner's *Fliegender Holländer*). Vampires certainly had a good run in the early 1800s: there was Silvestro de Palma's *I vampiri* (1812), Martin-Joseph Mengal's *Le Vampire* (1826) and above all Peter Joseph von Lindpaintner's *Der Vampyr* (1828), whose heroine, Isolde by name, falls under the sinister spell (in France, however, not Scotland) of Hypolit, the eponymous monster. (This opera originally had much spoken dialogue, as did *Der Freischütz*, but Lindpaintner later replaced this with recitatives.) Marschner would also achieve fame with his *Hans Heiling* (1833), with a libretto by Eduard Devrient, an opera originally intended for Mendelssohn, on an earth-spirit who, at the climax, turns an entire wedding party to stone. All very Gothic, all very much of its time, but we also find the emergence of complex, tormented and emotionally disturbed individuals – Heiling himself and also the Templar in Marschner's *Der Templer und die Jüdin* (The Templar and the Jewess) – whose anguished conflicts would not be out of place in Wagner.

His first purely musical compositions date from the middle of 1829; he had learned to play the piano adequately, had a few desultory harmony lessons and studied the technique of composition from books. He had once airily told his uncle that his play would not be constrained by mere pedantry; now, however, he was becoming increasingly aware of the need for more rigorous training, above all in what *he* wanted to do. The *Wagner Werk-Verzeichnis* lists sonatas, a string quartet, a handful of songs, a draft for a pastoral opera. At the end of 1830 he worked on a Concert Overture in B major which demanded that every fourth beat be marked by the intervention of a kettle drum. This was performed at the Leipzig Municipal Theatre on Christmas Eve and Wagner and his sister Ottilie were present when it was heard as part of a Declamatorium' where texts were recited, *tableaux vivants* enacted and pieces of music performed. The audience was obviously baffled by it and finally roared with laughter at the inevitable insistence of the drum. Incidentally, the Kapell-meister who organized these concerts was Heinrich Dorn, who had originally thought highly of Wagner and praised his devotion to Beethoven and the skill with which he copied out the full score of some of Beethoven's overtures, sonatas and quartets. He would later succeed Wagner as music director in Riga and grew increasingly antagonistic towards him, even trying to oust him by his own, risible *Die Nibelungen*.

In 1831, without having obtained a school leaver's certificate, Wagner – this now being his surname – matriculated at the University of Leipzig as a student who was ineligible for state examinations but was able to attend lectures.[6] There were predictable excesses – drinking and gambling – but Wagner also became, for six months, a conscientious pupil of Christian Theodor Weinlig, choirmaster at St Thomas's, who methodically taught him the basis of composition. Wagner would later praise the teaching of this kindly but strict mentor, his way of pointing out length and balance, principal modulations, the number and quality of themes and the general character of a movement; Weinlig regularly set exercises with precise instructions on what was to be done. It was these few months that set Wagner on a track which he found congenial and which he exploited fully after his fashion.

Up to his nineteenth year, Wagner's music, compared to that of, say, Mendelssohn, let alone the greater masters, is undistinguished, to say the least. But the breakthrough came in November 1832 with a performance of his Symphony in C major at the Conservatory in Prague. It is an accomplished display of controlled composition, demonstrating what he had learned and in such a short time: complete mastery over counterpoint and classical construction. An affinity with Beethoven's Second Symphony in D major is unmistakable and much of the orchestral colouring is reminiscent of Weber, but Wagner's own voice is certainly there in the melodious second movement and also in the exuberant Scherzo. The two concert overtures *König Enzio* (King Enzio), based on Ernst Raupach's play, and *Polonia* (inspired by the Polish uprising against Russia in 1830), likewise expelled the embarrassing memories of the 'Drumbeat' overture of 1830 most forcibly. Again, Beethoven may be detected in *König Enzio*, as can Cherubini, especially his overture to *Les deux journées*, frequently called *The Water Carrier*. (This work, incidentally, was praised by both Beethoven and Mendelssohn; Cherubini may also be said to anticipate Wagner by his use of the orchestra to heighten the dramatic moment and in writing music that was often declared to be unsingable). But it is in the later *Faust* overture (December 1839–January 1840) that we find Wagner promising to be the true master of symphonic form, a form which suited him admirably, and it is much to be regretted that the *Faust* symphony was never completed. Longing, pleading, grief and despair are adroitly portrayed, as is the heavy, oppressive atmosphere of doubt and hopelessness. At the very end of his life Wagner wished to turn again to one-movement symphonies, but it was too late; he did, however, some six weeks before his death in Venice, conduct his Symphony in C major in the Teatro la Fenice.

In his twentieth year Wagner knew that he must achieve fame and recognition as an opera composer, and his reading of Johann Gottlieb Büsching's *Ritterzeit und Ritterwesen* (The Age of Chivalry) provided him with an indispensable source of material for his work. He was drawn to a verse narrative by an anonymous thirteenth-century German poet to which the title 'Frauentreue' (The Devotion of Woman) had later been added. This, Wagner believed, would be his first operatic success. He gave it the title *Die Hochzeit* (The Wedding). A frenzied lover (Cadolt) climbs to the tower room of Ada, the fiancée of his friend Arindal, where she is virtuously waiting for her betrothed. She struggles with the madman and hurls him down into the courtyard, where every bone in his body is broken. At his funeral Ada suddenly utters a cry and sinks lifeless on to Cadolt's corpse.[7] In Büschinger's re-telling of the medieval tale, Wagner's 'frenzied love' had been a knight who, wearing only a silk shirt instead of armour, had been wounded in a tournament while championing the virtue of a lady: a spear had been embedded in his side and he would only allow this lady to remove it, which she does (are there shades of Amfortas or Parsifal here?). Later the knight enters the lady's bedchamber and forces himself on her; she, sleeping naked, manages to restrain him and dress in a silken nightgown. The struggle has opened the knight's wound and he bleeds, Tristan-like, to death. The lady secretly carries his body away and lays him in a coffin in church. Then, before the altar, she slowly undresses until she wears only a shift, before sinking lifeless on the knight's corpse. Wagner's projected opera seems very restrained indeed; he would later, in *My Life*, describe his fragment as being of blackest hue, without any operatic embellishment;[8] he had hoped that his sister Rosalie might use her influence and get it staged. She, apparently, hated it, finding the subject-matter unwholesome, and at Christmas 1832 he destroyed the various drafts, smarting under Rosalie's disapprobation and ridicule.

But his appetite had been whetted and, encouraged by Rosalie to find new material, he started writing his first fully completed opera, *Die Feen* (The Fairies), based on *La donna serpente* (The Serpent Woman), a story by Carlo, Count Gozzi. Wagner certainly knew E.T.A. Hoffmann's collection *Serapionsbrüder* (The Serapion Brethren, 1819–21), which included the narrative 'Der Dichter und der Komponist', a dialogue between a composer and a poet in which the idea of a 'musical drama' as 'Romantic opera' is mooted; music, we are told, must emerge directly from the poem as a necessary product of it, and Gozzi, whose fairy tale plays would provide suitable subjects for such an opera, is extolled (Adolf Wagner certainly knew his Gozzi and had translated him into German). In 1833 Wagner's Symphony in C major was played in the Gewandhaus and Wagner went to his brother Albert in Würzburg, where he took up the poorly paid post of chorus

The final apotheosis in an 1888 performance of *Die Feen*, Wagner's first full-length opera.

manager in the theatre; he started to compose music for *Die Feen*
and rehearsed Marschner's *Der Vampyr*, also Meyerbeer's *Robert le
diable*, with its remarkable finale in Act Three where the ghosts of
debauched nuns appear as if by magic from their graves (he also
provided a new tenor aria for his brother, who was singing the role
of Aubry in Marschner's work). But he worked feverishly on his own
opera, finishing the score in January 1834. He desperately wished
to see it performed in Leipzig, but the producer, Hans Hauser,
would not accept it. The world would have to wait until 1888 when
Hermann Levi conducted it in Munich, the cast including several
singers who had created roles in Wagner's later works. The musical
preparation was in the hands of Richard Strauss, and in the revival
of 1895 the role of Ada would be sung by Paula de Ahna, soon to
become Strauss's wife.

Two themes appear in the opera which would be very important
for Wagner: the collision between the spirit world and the world
of men, and the theme of redemption through love. These are
fundamental to his *oeuvre*, but apart from these *Die Feen* is a
curious piece which fits awkwardly into the Wagner canon. He
distanced himself from it; in *My Life* he speaks ironically about
the work, implying that the poetry was slapdash (can he *really* be
a poet?) and that he'd been a 'composer' simply for the sake of a
'libretto'.[9] It may also be true that he was making amends, so to
speak, for suggesting the irreconcilability of marriage and physical
passion in his sketches for *Die Hochzeit*, guiltily seeking to pacify
his family (and gain his sister's support) by glorifying conjugal love
and its triumph over supernatural machinations.

A brief synopsis is necessary as the opera is rarely performed
and relatively unknown. Before the curtain rises we are told that
Arindal, king of Tramond, encounters a particularly beautiful
doe while hunting and follows it into the night. With his servant
Gernot he mysteriously enters a fairy kingdom where, instead of a
doe, the beautiful Ada approaches him and he immediately falls in

love with her. (It should not be forgotten that Wagner greatly admired the plays of Ferdinand Raimund in which fantastic encounters between the worlds of fairies and of men frequently occur).[10] It may seem strange that Wagner should take over these names from *Die Hochzeit*; in all probability he wished to show that he had expunged the bizarre love triangle of the earlier work and was starting anew. Arindal marries Ada under the condition that for eight years he will not ask her who she is. The years pass and two children are born. Just before the expiry of the stipulated period of time Arindal does, in fact, pose the forbidden question; he is instantly separated from her, removed from the fairy kingdom and transported to a rocky, desolate landscape. The opera now opens with Ada summoned by the king of the fairies. She refuses to renounce her mortal husband and decides to leave the fairy realm for his sake and become a mortal herself. The king, however, attaches new requirements which Ada must fulfil. Now begin various trials which are highly reminiscent of *Die Zauberflöte*: when Ada approaches Arindal as a brutal, loathsome mother who suddenly pushes the two children into a fiery abyss, Arindal curses her, having previously been warned of the consequences of such an act. Immediately her actions are revealed as an illusion, but her husband's curse has turned her to stone (in Gozzi's tale she is turned into a serpent). The final act sees Arindal demented and wandering until, with shield, sword and lyre, he rallies to defeat those forces which were arraigned against him. Ada is saved from petrifaction by the sound of the lyre and the two, with their children, live happily ever after. The fairy kingdom does not relinquish Ada, but Arindal is elevated to the rank of the immortals.

A 'romantische Oper' indeed, and one which Wagner disavowed. If he *were* trying to curry favour with his family he was, perhaps, not being true to himself, and this a Richard Wagner could not contemplate. Yet there is much musical intensity in the work, certain prefigurations of what was to come later: a rudimentary use of the leitmotif, the portrayals of certain border states of consciousness and a very skilful mad scene in Act Three where Arindal hears the braying horns of the huntsmen in a state of delirium very reminiscent of Sieglinde's terror in *Die Walküre*. He also sees the dying glance of the doe as it is struck down by his arrow; this would recur again in *Parsifal* as the 'pure fool' looks at the swan he has just killed, seeing its dying gaze; Kundry will also speak of Christ's glance as she mocked Him. Most moving of all is Isolde's memory of how the stricken Tristan gazed up at her, and how his glance turned her vengeance to compassion.[11]

With plans for a possible production of *Die Feen* in Leipzig finally abandoned, Wagner lost interest in the work and underwent a surprising aesthetic volte-face. On 10 June 1834 his essay 'Die deutsche Oper' appeared in the *Zeitung für die elegante Welt* (Journal for Polite Society); in it the 21-year-old argues that 'we must seek to cultivate the age's 'new forms' (v, p. 12), turning our backs, presumably, on Romanticism. The editor of this journal, Heinrich Laube, was an acquaintance of Wagner's and one of the leading advocates of 'Junges Deutschland' (Young Germany), hardly a movement as such but an attitude of mind among young writers who drew their inspiration from the July Revolution in France in 1830. The term itself was first used by Ludolf Wienbarg in his *Ästhetische Feldzüge* (Aesthetic Skirmishes), a series of letters calling for the rejection of the pseudo-medievalism of the Romantic age and for an emphasis on contemporary life and its problems. Wagner endorsed this enthusiastically: he now loved the material world and attacked obscurantism and stultifying, puritanical morality. It is sensuous love which must now be praised; no more Germanic mysticism but the South with its love and joy. Wilhelm Heinse's novel *Ardinghello oder die glückseligen Inseln* (Ardinghello or The Blessed Isles, 1787), a portrayal of untrammeled joy and hedonism on the islands of Naxos and Paros, had been Laube's literary model and one which Wagner now shared. 'Die deutsche Oper' claimed that the Germans had neither a national German opera (even Weber is criticized) nor a national theatre; it is song that the Italians naturally had, and it is Bellini who is extolled. Elsewhere it would be Auber who was applauded, a composer praised by Wagner in his *Erinnerungen an Auber* (Reminiscences of Auber) for the dramatic quality of his scenes and for being able to write an entire act (Wagner is thinking of *La Muette de Portici*) which captures the audience's attention and holds it in thrall.

The fruit of his new attitude would be Wagner's next opera *Das Liebesverbot* (The Ban on Love), based very loosely on Shakespeare's *Measure for Measure*; Wagner reduced Shakespeare's twenty characters to five and of the seventeen scenes he took only four. In the summer of 1834 he was invited to act as musical director for a theatrical group during the summer season in Bad Lauchstädt; here he was able to put into practice his belief in sensuous gratification among the actresses and met one Wilhelmine 'Minna' Planer, four years his senior, and her younger 'sister' Natalie (in fact her illegitimate daughter by a guards captain who had seduced and abandoned Minna at the age of fifteen). In Bad Lauchstädt Wagner started the libretto of *Das Liebesverbot* and worked doggedly on the piece throughout the year, hoping to pay off certain debts he had incurred. The opera received its premiere on 29 March 1836 in Magdeburg; there had only been ten rehearsals and the result was predictable. The second performance, two days later, ended in uproar and fisticuffs among the actors due to a marital dispute. It would not be staged in Germany again until 1923; Britain would have to wait until 1965.

The action takes place in Palermo (to have set it, as Shakespeare does, in Vienna, where the Duke claims he has seen 'corruption boil and bubble/Till it o'er run the stew', might have caused difficulties among Metternich's censors). The governor Friedrich, ruling in place of the King, is portrayed as an inhibited German, hating sexual love and therefore reviled by the advocates of a new liberalism. His priggishness is totally at odds with Sicilian society till he, 'love's antidote', is consumed by passion for Isabella. Tormented by lust in such a setting, he strangely anticipates another who (and Wagner will find his magic garden in Ravello, near Naples) even castrated himself to extirpate sexual desires. Friedrich promises to spare the life of Claudio, Isabella's brother, if she will submit to him (he has already given orders for Claudio's execution). He will also sacrifice himself for this love; he will sexually enjoy Isabella's body, then die. 'Death and lust await me both.' Friedrich's lust and his reactionary laws show a deadening attitude to life and the people rise in revolt, and Claudio is released from prison. Friedrich desires death but the crowd, rejoicing, announce that the law is abolished and that they will show him every mercy. The opera ends in a wild celebration of life, freedom and sexual abandonment.

Is this, then, another youthful aberration? Wagner called it so when he presented the score to Ludwig II in 1866. But the young composer had learned much; there is some lively music, skilful ensemble and an assured handling of crowd scenes reminiscent of Auber and more than a hint of Italian *commedia dell' arte*. Bel canto, it seems, and French *opéra comique* have played their part: those who associate Wagner exclusively with ponderous German metaphysics may well be surprised when listening to this work. The use of the leitmotif is becoming more noticeable (the ban on love, for instance); Barry Millington has also pointed out pre-echoes of the Dresden Amen here (the nuns' 'Salve Regina') and echoes of Act Two of Beethoven's *Fidelio* in the prison scenes.[12] One wonders what would have become of Wagner had he continued in this vein, but he had other irons in his musical fire: he was feeling that he was now ready, now ripe enough for grand opera, and that only Paris would do for him.

In the meantime, however, he sought to have *Das Liebesverbot* performed in Berlin; he also hoped for a post in Königsberg and travelled there, also to Memel. Here he set about writing a grand historical opera, *Die hohe Braut oder Bianca und Guiseppe* (The High-born Bride; or, Bianca and Joseph), based on a novel by the popular novelist Heinrich Koenig, to be set in and around Nice in 1793. Laube had praised Wagner's historical reportage and Wagner (somewhat naively) believed that Eugène Scribe, the most prolific librettist of his day and a man who wielded enormous influence in Paris, might accept it. Wagner sent the libretto to Paris but received no reply; he also approached Meyerbeer. He had miscalculated: the rabble-rousing crowd scenes and revolutionary fervour (the opera finished with uproar, a riot, a stabbing, a suicide, cannon shots from the citadel, military music and the triumphant arrival of the French armies with the tricolor displayed with panache) were out of place after the establishment of the July monarchy. It seems that Wagner could not get Auber out of his mind, and grand spectacle haunted him, especially the death of Fenella, the heroine of *La Muette de Portici*, hurling herself into the streams of lava pouring from an erupting Vesuvius; Hérold's *Zampa* has Etna as an obliging volcano, also a stone statue on the finger of which the protagonist places a ring which he is later unable to remove. The work of Spontini also left a powerful impression; Wagner had seen the Italian, then Grand Music Director in Berlin, conduct his *Fernand Cortez ou La Conquête de Mexique* in 1836 and greatly admired the heavy scoring, especially for brass, the sensational effects (the cavalry charge, the massive ensembles, the burning of the Aztec temple) and the lyrical emotionalism of Amazily's love music. And he would later admit that it was Spontini who had guided him, above all in the conception of *Rienzi*.[13]

Having drawn a blank he turned to writing a comic opera, *Männerlist grösser als Frauenlist oder die glückliche Bärenfamilie* (Men's Cunning Outdoes Women's Cunning; or, the Bears' Happy Family, 1838), intending it to be an amusing counterpoint to *Die hohe Braut*; he took it from one of the tales of *The Arabian Nights* but transformed the action from Baghdad to contemporary Germany.

It was written in the style of French *opéra comique* with more than a dash of Rossini, but it remained little more than a sketch. Restless and generally dissatisfied with life – for Minna, whom he had married in 1836, was becoming increasingly moody and had now left him – he desperately sought a theme he could turn into ringing and triumphant music which must outdo the works so enamoured of the French (and of himself); his finances were also in a critical state and he dashed off the *Rule Britannia* overture in the hope of becoming known in London. It was when he was in Dresden's suburb Blasewitz in June 1837, when his marriage seemed almost lost, that he came across G. N. Bärmann's translation of Edward Bulwer-Lytton's novel *Rienzi, the Last of the Roman Tribunes*, which had appeared a few years before, and knew instinctively that this was *the* subject for him. He decided that he would attempt something so vast that only Europe's largest opera house could be capable of performing it; the plan would also be used 'to escape from the crushing limitations of provincial theatrical life in which he found himself and – of great interest psychologically – from a serious marital crisis with his first wife Minna which almost led to divorce'.[14] He would emulate and outdo the portrayal of the revolutionary hero Masaniello in *La Muette de Portici*, the ardent fervour of Eléazar's prayer in Halévy's *La Juive* (The Jewess) and the portrayal of Catholic pomp in the same opera (Cardinal Brogni's curse), as well as the conspiracy of the nobles in Meyerbeer's *Les Huguenots*; the ending would portray the destruction by fire of one of Rome's grandest buildings. Paris, then would be his.

When Wagner met Bulwer-Lytton's son in Vienna in the early 1860s he assured him that his father's novel had been his only source. There are striking resemblances, however, between Wagner's opera and a highly successful English play, *Rienzi* (1828), by Mary Mitford: in this play Rienzi's two careers, as Tribune and as Senator (separated in history and Bulwer's novel) are combined into one. It is also of interest that Rienzi, diverging from Bulwer-Lytton, is unmarried in Mitford and Wagner, a celibate figure exerting a more powerful charisma. But Bulwer's novel was certainly Wagner's main source and he skilfully converted the rambling work into an action-packed drama, complex and theatrically powerful. It should also be remembered that Rienzi 'was one of the first successful operas in the history of the genre to have a libretto written by the composer'.[15]

At the end of July 1837 Wagner took up the post of musical director in Riga, then part of the Russian Empire, and worked on the text and the music of *Rienzi*. But it was also here that he probably read Heinrich Heine's short story on the *Flying Dutchman* in the latter's *Aus den Memoiren des Herren von Schnabelewopski* (From the Memoirs of Herr von Schnabelewopski); Heine may have seen Edward Fitzball's melodrama *The Flying Dutchman; or, the Phantom Ship* during his stay in London earlier that year. In chapter Seven of his memoirs Schnabelewopski recalls seeing a play about the *Flying Dutchman* in Amsterdam. His enjoyment is interrupted at the point where Senta – in Heine's Scottish setting, Katharina – swears undying loyalty by pieces of orange peel dropped on his head, deliberately it would seen, by a beautiful young girl (*'eine wunderschöne Eva'*) sitting above him in the gods, or 'paradise'. The pair leave the theatre and enjoy an hour's dalliance on the couch. Schnabelewopski returns just in time to see 'Mrs *Flying Dutchman*' hurl herself into the sea. (We shall of course, meet another 'Eva' in paradise much later in Wagner's work.) It is remarkable that alongside conceiving scenes of pomp, power, tumult, bombast, fanfares and marches, Wagner should also brood on the lonely wanderer cursed to sail the seas forever. Had he subconsciously felt, sensed, that the world of German Romanticism *was* his true home, despite the blandishment of Parisian grand opera? But in Riga he worked on *Rienzi*, wrote enthusiastically on Bellini, learned French for four weeks (a language which he had contemptuously rejected at school)

The eponymous hero of Wagner's *Rienzi* (1838–40) enters Rome in triumph.

and accommodated a contrite Minna, who had returned from an escapade with a merchant called Herr Dietrich.

After failing to secure tenure in Riga (for which he blamed the malevolence of Heinrich Dorn), the Wagners moved in 1839 to Mitau (Courland); one of the last works Wagner conducted there was Weber's *Oberon*. But with creditors clamouring, Wagner took the decision to flee with Minna and his large Newfoundland dog Robber. Because Russian law demanded that applications for passports be listed in the local papers three times for the information of anyone who might have financial claims on the applicant, the flight would have to be illegal and clandestine. The Wagners, with Robber, went at night to the Russian border, which was patrolled by cossacks; they succeeded in crossing it by running down a hill and scrambling through a ditch until they reached Prussian soil. An accident in a farm cart not far from Königsberg left Minna badly injured and in need of rest (whether or not she suffered a miscarriage is uncertain). At Pillau, about 30 miles from Königsberg, they boarded a small boat with a seven-man crew, the *Thetis*, the captain having been prepared to take them without the necessary papers.

The journey to London, and thence Paris, has now become legendary; what would normally have taken eight days took some three weeks through storm and mountainous seas. Much later, in *My Life*, Wagner would describe the experience, telling us that the ship took refuge in a Norwegian fjord and a village called Sandvika near Arendal; there, with the crew's shouts echoing round the cliffs of granite, the creative inspiration for *Der fliegende Holländer* occurred (notwithstanding, as we know, the fact that the original draft had a Scottish setting). On arriving at Gravesend the German couple and their dog alighted and made their way to the great metropolis by river steamer, staying at the King's Arms in Old Compton Street. Determined to meet Bulwer-Lytton, Wagner presented himself in the House of Commons and enquired, probably in execrable English or appalling French, if he might

Giacomo Meyerbeer.

have an interview. On hearing that the novelist was not in town, Wagner had to content himself with visiting the Strangers' Gallery, where he saw the prime minister, Melbourne, and the Duke of Wellington himself. Wagner also visited Westminster Abbey and stood in deep reverence before the Shakespeare memorial until an impatient Minna pulled him away.

On 20 August they crossed to Boulogne-sur-mer; on the boat Wagner learned from an English lady that Meyerbeer himself happened to be in Boulogne and willingly provided Wagner with a letter of recommendation. The Wagners rented a villa just outside the town and Wagner hastened to visit the famous composer, who had just celebrated his 48th birthday and was basking in the success of *Les Huguenots* and *Robert le diable*. At this time Wagner admired Meyerbeer, a German composer who had been clever enough to take the Italians and the French as his models and beat them at their own game. Meyerbeer praised the music of the first two acts of *Rienzi*, which Wagner had just completed, and applauded the young German's neat calligraphy, calling it 'typically Saxon'. He promised to write letters of recommendation to the relevant authorities at the Paris Opéra. Wagner, swelling with pride, sensed that greatness was within his grasp. On 16 September he, Minna and the dog travelled by diligence to the capital. The city, he felt, would welcome him with open arms. He was to be bitterly disappointed.

2

Paris and Dresden

Paris – this 'femme entretenue of the world . . . ' How glad I am to be a German!

The two and a half years that Wagner spent in Paris, from September 1839 to April 1842, were years of hardship and disillusionment. The cocksure Saxon provincial learned to his cost that the musical world of Paris was supremely indifferent to his demands, that Meyerbeer's references had little effect and that the directors of the Opéra had other, more pressing concerns than those preoccupying Herr Wagner. The Conservatoire condescended to rehearse his *Columbus* overture but the piece was poorly received. In dire financial straits, Wagner pawned every object which might have had some value and was soon reduced to selling the pawn tickets. The Newfoundland dog disappeared, only to return the following year. One glimmer of light was a rehearsal which he heard at the Conservatoire of Beethoven's Ninth Symphony; here was German music at its greatest and the embittered 26-year-old, impoverished and resentful, wrote in his autobiographical sketch that he was completely dissatisfied with the Opéra, with its complete lack of anything approaching genius in its productions. Grapes, it seemed, had never been more sour. He set about writing the '*Faust*' Symphony and completed the overture in the following year.

He was leading a hand-to-mouth existence setting French poems to music (by Hugo, Ronsard and Jean Reboul); he also set Heine's

'Les deux Grenadiers'. The contact with Heine would be a fruitful one. Heine had been living in Paris since 1831 and wrote for the *Augsburger Allgemeine Zeitung* on the Parisian scene, including music. Wagner was keen to meet the man whose flippant version of the *Flying Dutchman* story had struck a deep chord within him. Heine would also give him the idea for *Tannhäuser* (Wagner would later seek to give the impression that he gained his themes from medieval sources, but modern versions also provided him with material). He copied Heine's witty and satirical style when he wrote his own articles for Maurice Schlesinger's *Revue et gazette musicale*; he was also able to write for the Dresden press and occasional pieces for Robert Schumann's *Neue Zeitschrift für Musik* (New Journal for Music) to keep his head, and that of his wife, above water. Meetings with Berlioz and Liszt (who was living in grand style and doubtless increased Wagner's envy) were memorable experiences.

As well as proofreading and similar hack work Wagner was composing the music for *Rienzi*; a ray of hope was the acceptance in March 1840 by the Théâtre de la Renaissance of his opera *Das Liebesverbot*. The Wagners, in anticipation of pecuniary alleviation, rented a larger flat; unfortunately the theatre was forced to close due to bankruptcy. Wagner also received through the post his *Rule Britannia*, which had been returned to him from London with a letter of regret and no postage paid; he had to send it back for lack of money. The situation became so serious that Minna had to lie in begging letters that her husband was in debtors' prison. Wagner was forced to sell the libretto of *Der fliegende Holländer* to the Opéra, where it was later used as the basis for an opera by two French rimesters which a certain Pierre-Louis Dietsch named *Le Vaisseau fantôme*. Dietsch would later, as we shall see, drive Wagner to distraction by his totally incompetent handling of the score of the Paris *Tannhäuser* performance in 1861; his *Vaisseau fantôme*, however, drew more on Captain Marryat and other sources than

Ernst Kietz's portrait of Wagner, drawn in Paris, *c.* 1840.

on Wagner, who felt that he had been treated shabbily (the money he received for the libretto, however, some 500 francs, was indeed welcome). It was remarkable that Wagner was able to work under such circumstances but sheer obstinacy and an unquenchable belief in his own greatness drove him on; he worked on Senta's ballad, on the songs of the Dutch and Norwegian sailors and also on the completion of *Rienzi*, finishing the musical score on 19

November 1840. The year ended in abject poverty and a wild party with their immediate friends who were as impoverished as the Wagners: Samuel Lehrs, a philologist, E. G. Anders, a German librarian working at the Bibliothèque nationale, and Ernst Benedikt Kietz, who would do the drawing of the young Wagner reproduced here.

At the beginning of 1841 Wagner's novella *Ein Ende in Paris* (A Death in Paris) appeared in three instalments in the *Revue et gazette musicale*. (It was praised by Berlioz in the *Journal des débats* and shown by him to Heine, who is reported to have said that E.T.A. Hoffmann could not have done better.) A narrator recounts his memory of the day he came across a magnificent Newfoundland dog bathing in the fountains of the Palais Royal; the dog's owner, we learn, is 'R'. This 'R', a German composer, has suffered and worked for his art alone and despises the blandishments of meretricious Paris. In subsequent meetings it becomes apparent that he is unwell; the narrator learns nothing more until a letter arrives with the admonition: 'Dear Friend, come and see me die.' With foreboding he hurries to Montmartre and climbs to a wretched attic where 'R' is expiring. He tells of his travails and of a base trick played by an arrogant Englishman who stole his dog from him. At the point of death he rallies and utters his creed: 'I believe in God, Mozart and Beethoven, likewise in their apostles and disciples; I believe in the Holy Ghost and in the truth of the one indivisible Art.' (This Art, of course, is music, the highest of all). He also, he whispers, believes in a Day of Judgment, to be visited upon those who have prostituted themselves for mere pelf, and also in the ultimate transfiguration of those who are Art's true disciples. 'R' dies young (as did Wilhelm Wackenroder's ficticious musician Joseph Berglinger) and at his funeral only the narrator and two mourners are present, a philologist and a painter. But the Newfoundland dog appears and lies by the graveside in true Greyfriars Bobby fashion; the snobbish

Englishman who had stolen him promises now to make amends by offering 50 guineas for a gravestone.[1]

We see an increasing bitterness in Wagner caused, obviously, by lack of recognition and of money. He believed that Meyerbeer's successes were due above all to the venality of the Opéra's directors and wrote to Schumann that Meyerbeer was a trickster ('*ein Betrüger*'). Before the Parisian premiere of *Der Freischütz* he explained the meaning of the work to the French and, after the performance, castigated them for their total lack of appreciation of German Romanticism. 'How lucky I am to be German!' he exclaimed in the *Dresdener Abendzeitung* of 24 June. And eight days later he received the news from the Royal Court Theatre in Dresden that its director, Baron August von Lüttichau, had graciously agreed to a performance of *Rienzi*. Both libretto and score had been completed in November 1840. On receiving von Lüttichau's letter, Wagner was determined that *Der fliegende Holländer* should also be staged and set himself the task of finishing the musical score in less than a month. He felt that he was now entering a new phase, one of revolutionary attack on the sterile artistic productions of his age. The score of his new opera was completed by mid-October; the Dutchman is seen as a fusion of Odysseus and the Wandering Jew, and the idea of redemption through a woman's love, treated flippantly in Heine, is now in deadly earnest.

The year 1841 ended in a great upsurge of energy: the hack work, a piano rendition of Halévy's *La reine de Chypre* (*The Queen of Cyprus*), was accomplished and there were many discussions with Samuel Lehrs on the immortality of the soul and on Feuerbach's *Das Wesen des Christentums* (The Meaning of Christianity), as well as on Proudhon's *De la propriété*, two seminal works that would affect Wagner deeply. At the very end of the year he planned an opera on Manfred, son of Frederick II, to be called *Die Sarazenin* (The Saracen Girl); the determination to succeed in Germany if the French did not deign to hear him grows ever stronger.

A fascinating prose sketch, *Die Bergwerke zu Falun* (The Mines of Falun), which Wagner wrote at the beginning of 1842 for 'a Jewish musician and composer not devoid of talent' was based on Hoffmann's story of the same name;[2] Wagner knew his Hoffmann well, and the image of the mine, the world of crystalline coldness, beauty and darkness juxtaposed with the realm of banal normal living, is a well known Romantic trope. Elis Fröbom is drawn to the fascinating subterranean world where the sinister Bergkönigin holds sway, and his beloved Ulla cannot save him. (Ludwig Tieck's *Der Runenberg* [The Mountain of the Runes] tells of a similar experience; Wagner frequently read this tale.) The world of normality on the one hand, with Elis's beloved Ulla, and that of the mountain queen on the other: this sketch of Wagner's, we notice, was written between the libretto of *Der fliegende Holländer* and the drafts for *Tannhäuser*, where another realm of artificial paradise would be portrayed.

On 2 April 1842 the Wagners (plus dog) left Paris and Wagner saw the Rhine for the first time. Passing the Wartburg in Thuringia, he sketched in his mind the Hörselberg scene from *Tannhäuser* and swore eternal fidelity to his German fatherland. Spring and summer would be taken up with rehearsals for *Rienzi* and attempts to get Berlin interested in *Der fliegende Holländer*; at the Schreckenstein near Aussig in northern Bohemia he began the first draft of *Tannhäuser*, then called 'Der Venusberg', that is, *mons veneris* (this title was later altered as it was pointed out that the *mons veneris* had indelicate connotations for the staff and students of the Saxon medical school in Dresden). The rehearsals for *Rienzi* dragged on, and Wagner despaired of ever seeing his grand opera on the stage: on 12 June 1842 he moaned to Samuel Lehrs that 'They are an accursed race, these Saxons, smarmy, clumsy, lazy and crude – what have I to do with them?' After seven weeks, on 20 October, the work was finally premiered in the Royal Saxon Court Theatre where, on 2 January 1843, *Der fliegende Holländer* would follow.

One month after this, Wagner was appointed the Royal Saxon Court's director of music (Kapellmeister). He had 'arrived', to the immense relief of his wife, who (mistakenly) believed that she and her husband could now look forward to a life of comfort and bourgeois respectability. The assistant conductor, also appointed at this time, was August Röckel, nephew of Hummel and brother-in-law of Lortzing; he became a social activist who would go on to found the revolutionary *Volksblätter* (People's Newspaper) with which Wagner would become associated some five years later with far-reaching consequences.

Let us pause here. *Rienzi, the Last of the Tribunes*, a 'grand tragic opera', Wagner's '*Schreihals*' or 'brawling brat' as he would later call it, was one of his greatest first-night successes. Wilhelmine Schröder-Devrient played Adriano and the famous tenor Joseph Tichatschek appeared in the title role; the performance lasted from six in the evening until well after midnight. The work is now rarely performed (and never in Bayreuth, as it is deemed to fall outside the accepted canon) but the overture, in classical form, is still heard as a concert piece: a long-held trumpet-call that signifies the struggle for freedom; an allegro dominated by the battle hymn and the theme of Rienzi's prayer; a lively gallop and the return of the blaring battle hymn as a brilliant coda. The opera is in two parts, Acts One and Two portraying Rienzi's might and the remaining three acts his undoing, hubris and death.

What brought Wagner to this figure? We know that Wagner was drawn very much to him after reading Bulwer-Lytton's novel in 1837; he wrote a letter to Joseph Tichatschek on 6/7 September 1841 begging him to accept the part of the hero:

The figure of Rienzi, as I imagined him and attempted to depict him, should be a hero in the full sense of the word, – a visionary dreamer who has appeared like some beacon of light among a depraved and degenerate nation whom he sees it as his calling to enlighten and raise up.[3]

Wagner also erroneously puts Rienzi's age at 28 at the time; he was actually 34 – as Wagner was himself when *Rienzi* was first accepted for performance in Dresden. Was there not a hint there that he sought to identify himself with this figure, thereby implying that he, Richard Wagner, was a young firebrand about to take the artistic world by storm? In *My Life* he describes how during rehearsals he believed that

> the whole crew in the theatre, right down to the humblest employees, loved me as if I were some sort of miracle and I am probably not far wrong in attributing much of this to sympathy for and interest in a young man whose difficult circumstances were all well known to them, and who was now to step from utter obscurity into sudden glory.[4]

Wishful thinking, perhaps, but Wagner would also become aware that Rienzi's overwhelming ambition, his visions of fame and limitless dominion (he appears in Act Two in outrageous and ostentatious robes), his fanaticism and his desire to change the whole of life utterly must necessarily lead to catastrophe. Rienzi would finally curse the Roman people who, he believed, had failed him, and his end, in conflagration and collapsing masonry, was somehow inevitable.

A fascinating work in many ways, not least because, as John Deathridge has told us, *Rienzi* is the first opera in the history of the genre in which a fruitful relationship was forged between text and music and a certain independence from formal operatic conventions was achieved. It is very much part of the 'tinsel world of nineteenth century opera', Deathridge tells us, yet somehow transcends it.[5] There is much Spontini in it, particularly in

'Rienzi's Might', a triumphant march that represents the supreme manifestation of power, of dramatic and emotional gesture; also, perhaps reminiscences of Spohr's *Jessonda* in the second half of the opera. 'Rienzi's Fall' is however more complex, and probes more deeply into the mind of the hero. The numerous processions and huge choruses do not glorify and praise so much as exemplify a downward curve; it is the *failure* of revolution that we see before us. It is possible that Wagner's later political pessimism is even prefigured here, that *Rienzi* is an early precursor of what would come much later. The flaming collapse of the Capitol, while paying service to the Opéra's more famous disasters (eruptions, bloodbaths, earthquakes and so on), perhaps anticipates the destruction of the hall of the Gibichungs in *Götterdämmerung* and concomitant catastrophes.

Rienzi is also tainted by its supposed connection with fascism. Hitler adored it and was given the original score which disappeared in the chaos of Berlin in 1945.[6] Well known is his claim, on reminiscing in 1939 about seeing a performance of the opera in Linz in 1906 or 1907, that 'In that hour it began!'[7] It was then that his new vision was born: that is, National Socialism. He had been carried away by the fanfares, banners, marches and flaming oratory, by the vision of one who rose from obscurity to reach the pinnacle of power; he did not seem to understand, in 1939, that destruction stood waiting in the wings. *Rienzi* was often revived in Berlin and Frankfurt after Hitler's rise to power in 1933; furthermore it should be remembered that the tenth anniversary of the Soviet Republic was also celebrated by a performance of the *Rienzi* overture in Moscow. It is strange that neither Hitler nor Stalin saw in the opera a 'devastating comment on the dynamics of totalitarianism'.[8] Wagner most certainly did but having at last triumphed on the Dresden stage, he had other, more haunting preoccupations.

We suggested in the introduction (and Wagner also made the claim) that there had been no other artist who had made such a remarkable transformation in so short a time as he. And it is indeed astonishing. No sooner had he finished *Rienzi* than he had almost completed *Der fliegende Holländer*, the one written in emulation of Parisian grand opera, the other a yearning for redemption and ultimate fulfilment in death. A greater contrast can scarcely be imagined. He had read Heine's story in Riga in 1838, yet did not write a sketch for a libretto until two years later. A full year was to elapse before he wrote the text in its final form, then he composed the music in the space of seven months, leaving only the orchestration and the overture to be completed in the winter of 1841. The 'bawling brat' may have made his name in Dresden, enabling him to hold his head high in the country of his birth, but *Der fliegende Holländer* was ultimately to show the world where his true genius lay. His imagination had been first fired by Heine's account of the Ahasuerus of the ocean and by his own experience of a stormy sea voyage and the cries of the sailors; he would now write music that outdid Mendelssohn in its portrayal of the sea. And the theme of redemption through love he would make quintessentially his own: a theme which would have appeared in his '*Faust*' Symphony, a 'Gretchen' theme, would become subsumed under the music of another redemptrix of a Faust-like figure roaming the seas.

He had hoped that the work would be staged in Berlin immediately after Meyerbeer's *Les Huguenots* but Berlin prevaricated and he had to accept Dresden. The premiere, we know, was on 2 January 1843 with Wilhelmine Schröder-Devrient as Senta; it was a failure and withdrawn after four performances, the audience disappointed and desirous of seeing more extravagant and rousing works like *Rienzi*. This was no more *melodrame à grand spectacle* but a sombre sea-girt setting, a strange reflective dream, weird elemental cries and much brooding on death and redemption. (Yet the steersman's lovely expression of his longing for his maiden, Wagner's homage to the bel canto of Bellini, perhaps, must surely have been applauded.) A reversal to Romantic opera, then, to *Der Freischütz*, *Der Vampyr* or even *Robert le diable*? Not quite, for it is a work of transition, overshadowing them by its dramatic force and the genius of the music. It was Wagner's self-identification with his central character, H. F. Garten would succinctly argue, 'which made him for the first time a poet and which made *Der fliegende Holländer* the first truly Wagnerian opera in its complete fusion of drama and music'.[9] There are also undeniable anticipations here of the death wish of Tristan and Isolde in the rapt isolation of the Dutchman and Senta, remote from quotidian realities; also in Senta's outburst, in extreme ecstasy, that she must die with him.

Weltschmerz, an outsider, a wanderer, an accursed one – these are the common themes in European literature at this time, of which Coleridge's 'The Rime of the Ancient Mariner' is a precursor. But the psychological intricacies of the Dutchman's tortuous longings are unique, and a writer of Thomas Mann's stature was amazed by them. In his celebrated lecture commemorating the fiftieth anniversary of Wagner's death, *Leiden und Grösse Richard Wagners* (Wagner's Suffering and Greatness), Mann draws our attention to the Dutchman's reaction on seeing Senta for the first time. He sings the following words:

> This sombre glow which I am feeling here,
> Should I then, wretched man, speak now of love?
> Oh no, of yearning, of redemption more;
> O let this angel bring it unto me! (ii, p. 29)

Thomas Mann explains that these lines are certainly singable, but never before, he insists, has such intellectually complex, spiritually convoluted material been sung:

> The damned one has fallen in love with this girl at first sight, but he tells himself that his love is not really for her, but for salvation. But now she stands before him as an incorporation of the possibility of salvation so that he is not willing, or able,

to differentiate between the longing for spiritual salvation and the longing for her. For his hope is now enshrined in her form and he cannot wish her to have another, that is, he loves the girl in redemption itself.[10]

It is hardly any wonder, we feel, that Michael Wächter, who sung the part of the afflicted wanderer, was all at sea; Wilhelmine, however, who had sung in Wagner's works before, had an inkling of what this revolutionary work had to say and acted Senta well, especially her ecstatic trance-like ballad. Wagner may well have been disappointed to see his new opera with its superb orchestration (Michael Tanner praises above all the 'raging first pages . . . in D minor, the demonic key of Mozart and Beethoven'[11]), masterful handling of the chorus, deep metaphysical brooding and remarkable portrayal of the trance state removed from the repertoire in favour of *Rienzi*, but he knew full well that the path he was taking, from history to myth, was the right one. And this opera alone now puts him in the ranks of the truly great.

In 1851, in his apologia pro vita sua *Eine Mitteilung an meine Freunde* (A Communication to my Friends), the indefatigable self-publicist in exile, ever desirous of hammering home to his listeners and readers in an overtly didactic fashion what his new, revolutionary works were all about, maintained that the figure of the Dutchman was a synthesis of Odysseus, Ahasuerus and Columbus (VI, p. 237): the first was Hellenic, the second Judeo-Christian and the third post-medieval, that is, modern. In antiquity one's longing was for one's homeland; in the Middle Ages it was for death; in the modern age it was for the *new*. This search for the new, however, is ultimately transformed into a longing for oblivion, a return to Ahasuerus, but death – release – is denied the Wandering Jew. Now death and redemption can only be vouchsafed through a woman who sacrifices herself out of love for the tormented soul. This woman is no longer Penelope sitting

The final scene of *Der fliegende Holländer* (1840–41) from the *Illustrierte Zeitung* of 7 October 1843.

by the hearth; she is '*the woman of the future*' (VI, p. 238). A nebulous concept indeed, but one which hovered before Wagner at this time. Interesting is the notion of the modern, 'absolute' artist as a homeless wanderer, one who seeks not domestic security but some transfigured state of mystical rapture. This 'absolute artist' is seen as a seafarer – and for Wagner the sea would always represent the essence of music, surging, sighing and oceanic. The Dutchman finds rest there in death, but only after Senta has joined him, hurling herself into the waves.

A month after the premiere of *Der fliegende Holländer* Heinrich Laube published Wagner's first attempt to explain to a startled world what he was and what he intended to do; *Eine Mitteilung an meine Freunde*, however, is a far more detailed account from a much more mature composer. In 1843 Wagner was installed as Royal Saxon Court Kapellmeister and had his audience with the king. In March he conducted the first performance of Gluck's *Armide* and jotted down the original draft of *Tannhäuser*; in the summer there occurred the first performance of his *Liebesmahl der Apostel* (*The Agape of the Apostles*), a vast oratorio for 1,200 male voices and a 100 musicians. Being also conductor of the local choral society, the *Liedertafel*, Wagner was obliged to write an oratorio for a singing festival featuring all the male voice choirs in Saxony; he dashed off the piece at high pressure and wrote for three large four-part choirs of disciples and a small choir of basses. He dedicated the work to the widow of the erstwhile cantor of St Thomas's, C. T. Weinlig, to whom Wagner felt a sincere debt of gratitude. It is now almost banished to obscurity; Wagner initially claimed that it was a great success but later brushed it aside. Be that as it may, we do, at least, hear pre-echoes of the as yet unwritten *Lohengrin*, even of *Parsifal*, in the voices from above and the descent of the Holy Ghost, a broad and triumphant melody.

During the summer Wagner repaired to Teplitz, where he immersed himself in Jakob Grimm's *Deutsche Mythologie* and began composing the music for *Tannhäuser*. On his return to Dresden, and a move to a more commodious dwelling, he began to build up a systematic library with an emphasis on Old Norse and medieval German literature. It may be argued that no musician has read more and written more than Wagner; that he is unique in musical history in his knowledge of literature both of past ages and his own time. This Dresden library, built up over seven years, then necessarily abandoned after his flight into exile, demonstrated his need to absorb the Greeks, Old French, English, Welsh and Spanish poetry, Dante, Byron, Goethe and Schiller, Lessing, *A Thousand and One Nights* and German fairy tales, to name but a few.[12] He also threw himself energetically into plans for reorganizing the musical life of Dresden, which inevitably led to tensions between him and the theatre manager's office; he also set his mind on convincing Berlin that it needed to experience his latest opera, which had not been the success in Dresden that he had hoped.

At the beginning of 1844 he had his way: Berlin agreed and on 6 January Wagner travelled to the Prussian capital. The Berlin premiere of *Der fliegende Holländer* took place under his baton on the following day in the presence of William IV. After the performance Mendelssohn congratulated him and Wagner believed that this momentous evening would be a turning point in his life. But the critics were again hostile and, back in Dresden, he took up work on the orchestral sketch for Act One of *Tannhäuser* with grim determination. Liszt, who was having an affair with the actress Lola Montez, visited him and requested a performance of *Rienzi* which Wagner organized; Hamburg also wished to see it. It was galling for Wagner to be reminded of his 'brawling brat' when his brain was full of plans for *Tannhäuser*. It was no longer 'grand opera' which interested him but something different; no longer 'effects without causes' but an authentic fusion of music and drama. But occasional pieces had to be written as his contract demanded: in August he composed a musical greeting to Friedrich August II on his return from England, in which an anticipation can be heard of the grand march in the Act Two of *Tannhäuser* ('Landgraf Hermann heil!'). More important for him was the commemoration of the return from London of Weber's mortal remains to Dresden. Wagner had insisted on this ceremony and forced it through despite considerable opposition. He composed a piece for male voice choir, also funeral music based on themes from *Euryanthe*. On 14 December Weber's body was conveyed from the banks of the Elbe to the Catholic cemetery in Friedrichstadt to the accompaniment of Wagner's solemn music for 80 wind instruments. On the following day he held a funeral oration at the graveside to the strains of his chorus 'Hebt an den Sang' (Let Song Resound); two weeks later he would finish the orchestral sketches for *Tannhäuser*'s third act.

The summer of 1845 would prove to be one of the most fruitful in Wagner's entire life in that the seeds were sown from which would blossom nearly all of his mature works. With wife, dog and parrot, Wagner travelled to Marienbad for a summer break, taking with him the works of Wolfram von Eschenbach (*Parzifal*) in Simrock's edition, the anonymous epic *Lohengrin* with Görres's introduction and the history of German literature by Gervinus. Here he would come across an account of Hans Sachs and the mastersingers of Nuremberg with their arcane formulations and rigid rules. Sachs, Wagner would tell us in *Eine Mitteilung an meine Freunde* (VI, p. 259), appeared to him as 'the last manifestation of the people's artistic productivity', and on a walk he would conceive the amusing scene where Sachs marks the pedantic marker's error with the hammer on his last. On 16 July he wrote a prose sketch of the three acts of *Die Meistersinger* containing those last famous lines, the declaration that, should the Holy Roman Empire dissolve into mist, then holy German art would prevail. (He was not to know that it would be some 23 years later that he would stand in the royal box of a king born that summer and receive rapturous acclamation for the glorious music of this masterpiece.)

On 19 October 1845 the premiere of *Tannhäuser und der Sänger-krieg auf Wartburg* (*Tannhäuser and the Minstrels' Contest on the Wartburg*) took place in Dresden with Joseph Tichatschek in the title role and the redoubtable Wilhelmine Schröder-Devrient as Venus; Wagner's niece Johanna sang the part of Elisabeth (she would later sing the part of Schwertleite, a Valkyrie, in the first Bayreuth production of *Die Walküre* in 1876). (There is, incidentally, another *Tannhäuser* by Carl Amand Mangold, a Darmstadt composer, which was started within one month of Wagner's and completed within eight days of his, although Mangold's was premiered in Darmstadt on 17 May 1846. It was, apparently, a greater success at the time than Wagner's but was then over-taken and ended in obscurity.) As with *Der fliegende Holländer*, the reaction was lukewarm at best. The public scarcely understood what they had seen and heard; a psychological drama had unfolded before them portraying the collision between sacred and profane love, but its resolution seemed unclear. Before having seen the opera, Schumann wrote in a letter to Mendelssohn on 22 October 1845 that Wagner had written yet another opera and that he was incapable of writing four successive bars of good, let alone beautiful, music (after seeing it he did, however, recant). The press spread the rumour that Wagner was in the pay of the Catholic party to propagate the doctrines of absolution and redemption. Wagner felt that he had been completely misunderstood and certainly not appreciated in contemporary Dresden. With his characteristic energy and resilience, however, four weeks later he invited an audience to listen to a reading of the libretto of his *Lohengrin* in the 'Engelsklub' ('Club of Angels'), a room set aside for various functions in a Dresden hotel.

Tannhäuser . . . The work would haunt him for the rest of his life; had he lived longer it would most certainly have been staged by him in his Festspielhaus, sensing as he did that there was something flawed in it which he must correct despite its wondrous moments: the transformation between Venusberg and Thuringian countryside in Act One, Elisabeth's greeting to the hall in Act Two and Tannhäuser's searing account of his journey to Rome in Act Three, a masterful fusion of dramatic recitation and arioso (it was first produced in Bayreuth by Cosima in 1891. A memorable production with several horses and a pack of 32 hounds was staged by Wagner's son Siegfried shortly before his death in 1930, and conducted by Arturo Toscanini).

It is unlikely that Wagner knew the medieval mystery plays of one Robert who, after a life of debauchery and crime, journeys to Rome to receive papal absolution: Meyerbeer's *Robert le diable* is based very loosely on this. He had found references to the minstrels' contest in E.T.A. Hoffmann's *Serapionsbrüder* compilation (1819–21), also Ludwig Bechstein's *Die Sagen von Eisenach und der Wartburg* (Legends of Eisenach and the Wartburg, 1815); more importantly

Photogravure print of Jacques-Clément Wagrez, *Tannhäuser's Flight*, 1896.

he was again indebted to Heine, in this case to the essay 'Element-argeister' (Elemental Spirits) which appeared in the third volume of *Der Salon* in 1837. Heine in turn was in thrall to Ludwig Tieck, acknowledged 'Father of German Romanticism' whose short story 'Der getreue Eckart und der Tannenhäuser' (Faithful Eckart and

the Knight Tannenhäuser) had appeared in 1797. In it the kind,
faithful Eckart stands guard outside the Venusberg situated in
the Hörselberg in Thuringia to which triumphant Christianity
had banished pagan idols, including Venus herself, a voluptuous
temptress, and warns men of the dangers which lurk within. Wagner
cleverly links the two legends – the singing contest on the Wartburg
and the dangerous proximity of the Venusberg – and it is here that
the Knight Tannhäuser, fleeing the sterile puritanism of the court,
will seek sexual gratification.

The overture portrays strikingly the contrast between the
solemn piety of the pilgrims and the chromatic sensuousness of
Venus and her cohorts as we are projected into a world of libidinous
excess. But Tannhäuser's first words as he starts up in Scene Two
are '*Zuviel! Zuviel!*' ('Too much! Too much!') Outsiders such as he
seek the emancipation of the flesh, either in the Isles of the Blessed
or Palermo or here, in the '*wärmenden Schoss*', the warming lap or
bosom of Venus's world. Yet now he tires of lubricious dalliance in
this artificial paradise; like the Dutchman he tires of the endlessness
of existence and, in the Paris version of the work, bluntly tells
Venus that he longs for death: '*O Göttin, woll' es fassen, mich drängt
es hin zum Tod*' ('Oh goddess, can't you see – it is for death I yearn').
Away, then, from endless, vacuous repletion, from warmth of womb
or breast to an awareness of transience, of pain even, to a more
Christian spirituality? But sensuality and spirituality can be strangely
interwoven: Wagner wrote an enlightening letter to Kietz comment-
ing on the Virgin's sexual attraction in which he describes the effect
of a copy of Carlo Dolci's *Madonna Addolorata*, an 'extraordinarily
affecting' painting which he had seen in Aussig; he also suggests
that if Tannhäuser had seen it, he, Wagner, could well understand
why he turned from Venus to Mary without being inspired by any
great sense of piety.[13] A miraculous transformation follows, to the
freshness of natural beauty and a shepherd piping to greet the
advance of spring.[14] Recognized by his erstwhile fellow knights,

Aubrey Beardsley's depiction in 1898 of *Tannhäuser's Return to the Venusberg*.

Tannhäuser is led, to the accompaniment of exultant hunting horns in joyful anticipation, to the great hall of the Wartburg where Elisabeth, the Landgrave's niece, will joyfully greet him.

The opening of Act Two is a moving portrayal of her joy, her agitation, her longing to see him who had been missing for so long, and her rapturous greeting of the empty hall leaves us in no doubt of her love for him: the music here is as intensely emotional as anything in the Dresden Venusberg. Elisabeth may be an object of veneration to the emotionally retarded knights of the Wartburg but she is a passionate woman who longs to hear Tannhäuser's voice again. His songs, she tells him after he has entered and fallen at her feet, awakened strange, new feelings within her breast, while those of the other minstrels were insipid and melancholy. After the great ceremonial entry of the Landgrave and the court it will be her task to give the victor in the song contest the prize and she longs to bestow it on the man she loves. The songs from the minstrels are indeed worthy, full of stilted praise of chastity. Walther von der Vogelweide (the historical German minstrel) might well, later, inspire Walther von Stolzing in *Die Meistersinger* to passionate emotionalism but here he can only sing of moderation and advise Tannhäuser to cool his heart at the spring of virtue. After Wolfram's worship of ideal devotion Tannhäuser begins his praise of physical love; there is silence in the hall. We notice that Elisabeth makes a movement to show her approval, but as the rest of the court exudes stony disapprobation she controls herself. And after the climactic praise of sexuality with which Tannhäuser's song ends, and his drunken praise of the Venusberg, she shows great courage and interposes her body between the deranged man and the knights who threaten to kill him.

Tannhäuser's love, his yearning for physical fulfilment, for sexuality (*not* literally the Hörselberg and its grotto, but as a symbol for erotic satisfaction), his desire for Elisabeth's femininity, suddenly become sinful. Elisabeth could have been his prize as she bravely protects him after his insane outburst, an outburst caused by disgust at the pallid platitudes he had just heard. But now, suddenly, it is his desire for *her* which is seen as sinful and she, after the disaster at the end of Act Two, is expected to play the role of divine intercessor, a Virgin Mary; she will become 'holy'. Tannhäuser had projected on to her his erotic desires – this is now his sin, not his earlier dalliance in the *mons veneris* (which had, we know, proved too much for him). He declaims this to the shocked disorientated gathering:

To guide the sinner to salvation
The god-sent woman came to me;

But oh, to touch her sinfully
I raised my lusting gaze to her (II, pp. 78–9).

In a letter to Franz Liszt on 29 March 1852 Wagner spelled this out
quite clearly: 'All his [Tannhäuser's] suffering, his bloody pilgrimage, everything stems from the idea contained in these lines.'
Tannhäuser, sunk in evil, rejected the 'herald of God's grace'; if
we do not understand this, Wagner implies, then Tannhäuser will
remain incomprehensible, a wanton, vacillating, pitiful figure.[15]
But Wagner's need to insist on this interpretation surely betrays
his fear that he has sacrificed Elisabeth, a loving, spirited and
courageous woman, for the sake of this unconvincing hero; she now,
in Act Three, prays, dies and becomes sanctified in order that the
papal staff should blossom and that Tannhäuser find salvation.[16]
She is carried in an open coffin across the stage; he expires and,
as the sun rises, the young pilgrims sing a joyous hymn to God's
merciful forgiveness. The sonorous chords of the pilgrims' chorus
bring this flawed yet fascinating opera to an exultant close.

Tannhäuser, it seems, looks backwards to the erotic freedom
extolled in *Das Liebesverbot* and forwards to the renunciatory ethos
of *Parsifal*. And Wagner, writing to his friend August Röckel on
23 August 1856, would, now in a deeply Schopenhauerian mode,
talk of the lofty tragedy of renunciation which Tannhäuser now
exhibits as an expression of 'the uniquely redeeming denial of the
will'.[17] But when we recall that amazing, highly charged bacchanal
which Wagner would compose for the Paris performance of 1861,
a bacchanal which overwhelmed Baudelaire, who found the 'whole
onomatopoeic dictionary of love' in it,[18] we surely feel uncertain as
to whether Wagner had succeeded in expunging the 'horrors' of
the Venusberg (see the letter to Mathilde Wesendonck, 10 April
1860) still exerted a baleful attraction.

Back, then, to Dresden and the life of Kapellmeister, with its
strains and frustrations. *Eine Mitteilung an meine Freunde* tells of

the worthlessness of the musical life in the city and of the failure of society at large; a radical change is needed. His restlessness is becoming more and more apparent, and a letter of 23 November 1847 to Ernst Kossak, a German philologist and journalist, speaks openly of 'the need to break the dam' which inhibits true liberty, the means being – 'Revolution!'[19] He sought solace, as so often, in Beethoven and in the spring of 1848 he conducted the Third, Fifth and Seventh Symphonies. In February revolution broke out in Paris; the Communist Manifesto appeared. On hearing that revolution had also broken out in Vienna, Wagner recklessly penned a 'Greeting from Saxony to the Viennese' which exulted in revolutionary fervour and greeted its insurgents joyfully; it appeared under his name in the *Allgemeine Österreichische Zeitung*. On 15 March the citizens of Dresden took to the streets, and the revolution that he had longed for seemed about to begin.

3

Revolution, Exile and Reform

You say I was mad to have broken the bridge to Dresden behind me?
You're wrong: *I* didn't break the bridge – it collapsed with a gigantic
crash behind me because it was badly built and rotten. It led me back
to a place in which I would have suffocated had I stayed.

The uprisings in Dresden in March 1848 were but a prelude to
the violence that erupted in May 1849. In 1848 the Saxon king
grudgingly agreed to the abolition of state censorship and to
reform the judiciary, electoral processes and taxation, and the
populace welcomed these and cheered His Majesty. There were
battles elsewhere, in Berlin and Frankfurt am Main, where meas-
ures were being taken to elect a National Assembly. And Wagner?

We have noticed his restlessness in the 1840s and his growing
need to align himself with any movement which would bring about
change. He was in his mid-thirties and becoming increasingly aware
that new directions were needed in his life and work. *Tannhäuser*
had not met with the acclaim he had hoped; he had finished the
score of *Lohengrin* on 28 April 1848 but saw little chance of its
being staged. The post of Hofkapellmeister he found increasingly
irksome. He found many of the operas he had to conduct trivial,
considering that they failed to explore the psychology and emotions of the characters and neglected the importance of dialogue,
of *drama*, above all. The relationship with his wife was becoming
increasingly strained and his financial position was becoming

increasingly parlous (a generous loan from Wilhelmine Schröder-Devrient had – surprisingly – to be repaid). When he finally did receive a rise in salary von Lüttichau humiliated him by writing in a report that he, Wagner, had adopted a frivolous attitude to his duties and did not appreciate his good fortune. It is therefore not surprising that Wagner should welcome the insurgents not primarily from a political standpoint but as a manifestation of a general desire for a new way of looking at the world.

On 11 May he penned a *Plan for the Organization of a German National Theatre for the Kingdom of Saxony* containing many valid ideas for theatrical reform, including a drama school and a more democratic structure in the election of committees; it was ignored. In a letter to the Saxon deputy of the new Frankfurt Parliament Wagner put forward a suggestion that the new National Assembly restrict *inter alia* the power of the German princes. In July he spoke at the left-wing Vaterlandsverein (Society for the Fatherland) on the relationship between republicanism and the monarchy; he attacked the 'demonic concept of money' together with bankers and speculators, the evil of interest rates and 'paper-swindling': all this must be swept away in order that true humanity should emerge. He could not, however, accept the 'senseless, tactless doctrine of communism' and insisted that the king should remain as the head of republican aspirations (he had, interestingly enough, met the Russian anarchist Michael Bakunin, who had fled from Prague and found shelter with August Röckel. Bakunin was certainly a colossal figure whose insistence on destruction, however, Wagner could not accept at this time). This speech of Wagner's appeared in print in a supplement to the *Dresdener Anzeiger*; it did not bear Wagner's name, but the authorities correctly guessed who had written it and *Rienzi* was removed from the programme of the Royal Saxon Court Theatre.

Wagner's prodigious energy and his powerful need to assert himself and strike out in a new direction is seen in various dramatic

Franz Liszt conducting *Lohengrin*, 1850.

projects linked, in some way or another, to various revolutionary ideas.[1] Before looking at these, *Lohengrin* must be considered. It was a work finished in April 1848 but not performed until 1850 under Liszt's baton in Weimar, on Goethe's birthday, while Wagner and his wife sat in the hotel Zum Schwan (The Swan) in Lucerne. This work is frequently passed over as an example of Wagner's 'early' period; it is in fact a masterpiece of orchestration, an example of his theatrical genius and a new beginning, thoroughly *durchkomponiert* with new harmonic procedures and vocal forces that go far beyond *Tannhäuser*. The shimmering A major chords of the prelude reminiscent of silvery, gossamer threads of almost luminous beauty leave an indelible impression; the divided violins giving an ethereal frisson. A major is the key associated always with the figure of Lohengrin and with the Grail, and this prelude portrays a vision of rapt transcendence and the materialization of the holy vessel with its descent into the world of men (II, pp. 201–2). The trumpet calls and festive ceremonies which Wagner does so well are here exemplary (and would later delight and captivate a young Bavarian king); the great strength of the work is undoubtedly the chorus, almost modelled on those of Greek tragedies in its comment and reaction. Wagner had also learned from Gluck that music must support poetry and strengthen emotional expressiveness without disturbing it by useless ornamentation,[2] and in *Lohengrin* there is indeed a perfect fusion of music and speaking line. There may still be vestiges of grand opera, but the associative use of tonality and the richness of orchestration show that Wagner was now an absolute master, a man who had thought very deeply about the problematic nature of the work.

We recall his reading in that fruitful summer of 1845 the anonymous epic on Lohengrin; he would also find references in Wolfram's *Parzival* to the hero's son Loherangrin. But increasingly Wagner conceived the legend in his own image, an image based on a palimpsest of Germanic legend upon classical archetypes. He saw the story as a timeless myth, a variation on the theme of Zeus and Semele. The god approaches Semele in radiant human form (not as bull, swan or shower of golden rain); despite his warning, and egged on by a jealous Juno, she experiences his blinding, divine brilliance and is immediately incinerated. But Wagner probes deeper.

The figure of Lohengrin can be seen to a certain extent as an outsider, similar to the Dutchman or to Tannhäuser, a typically Romantic figure, not at home in the world. Yet they are both redeemed by a woman's love; Lohengrin is not. He is not separated from this love by a curse or some baleful temptress but by his own elevated status: he is Parsifal's son and member of the community of the Grail. It is not the self-sacrificing love of a woman that can save him: he descended from his ethereal realm in answer to a cry for help. Is he not a knight in shining armour? Whatever else he is – and Wagner, in a letter, calls him a 'metaphysical phenomenon' – his tragedy is that the possibility of love was, tantalizingly, opened to him, but Elsa, tormented by doubts encouraged by Ortrud's dark insinuations, asks the forbidden question and forces him to return to Monsalvat.[3] Ortrud is certainly vanquished by Lohengrin's prayer, and the young Gottfried is returned to Brabant, but Elsa sinks lifeless before us.

Elsa is in the same mould as Senta, as Elisabeth – but these two redeemed the men they loved, while Elsa does not. Lohengrin could have been released from his metaphysical status – that is, made human – if she had not doubted, had not questioned him. Wagner knows that it is human nature for a woman to wish to know everything about her beloved, and Ortrud's vindictiveness ensures that the fatal question will be asked. Ortrud is a fascinating character, pagan and noble in appearance (her husband Friedrich von Telramund is reduced to the role of a mere accessory). She calls on the gods Wodan and Freia to supplant Christian virtues and to bless her cunning; she is black, Elsa white. With her key of F sharp minor she dominates Act Two and has a terrible majesty about her,

Lohengrin's arrival on the swan-boat, in a 19th-century print.

but she is also deeply flawed. In a letter to Liszt Wagner explains
that Ortrud is a woman *who does not know love* (his italics); this,
he explains, says it all.[4] Her nature, he explains, is conditioned by
the world of politics (the removal of Gottfried and the elevation of
Telramund and herself); a male politician, Wagner insists, disgusts

'Lohengrin's Departure', a postcard reproduction after a painting by Franz Stassen.

Margaret Ober as Ortrud.

us, yet a female politician is something appalling. Her only love, he concedes (for a woman must love something), is for ancestral pride, for power, and this love becomes murderous fanaticism, a terrible madness which can only be satisfied by the destruction of others – and herself. A tragic, searing work, then, despite the ever popular wedding march; the stirring pageantry and faith in Germanic might and power to crush the hordes from the East would also appeal later to more dubious elements.[5]

In 1852 Wagner spoke disparagingly of politics. Four years previously, however, he was described by Eduard Hanslick in Vienna as being up to his ears in politics and desperate to bring about all sorts of reforms, not only in opera but in all theatrical institutions and, indeed, the whole of society itself. We have noted his close collaboration with August Röckel, but Wagner's stance in those years of revolution differed from Röckel's in that the latter sought amelioration within an identifiable political framework whereas Wagner's vision became increasingly utopian, mystical even – and nationalistic. That he should share in the growth of German nationalism in the early years of the nineteenth century should not surprise us; deprived of the last vestiges of political cohesion with the dissolution of the Holy Roman Empire in 1806, Germany looked to its cultural heritage as a rallying point, and the literary works of the Middle Ages were hailed as a monument to a glorious past.[6] It was above all the *Nibelungenlied*, the great Middle High German epic poem, that came to the fore after being brought to the attention of a wider reading public in the plays of Friedrich de la Motte Fouqué (who had been friendly with Wagner's uncle Adolf) and Ernst Raupach. The editor of the *Neue Zeitschrift für Musik* had in 1845 expressed the view that a setting of the Nibelung material as an opera would be a 'step forward' and explained that 'the composer who could accomplish this task in an adequate manner would become the man of his era'.[7] We do not know whether either Wagner or writers like Friedrich Theodor Vischer and Louise Otto-Peters, who had both suggested something similar, read this; what we *do* know is that it was Wagner who would triumphantly provide the world with one of the most gigantic achievements in musical history on this very topic.

The years between 1848 and 1853 were a veritable maelstrom of frenetic activity for Wagner, though – surprisingly, given that he was renowned for works of epic grandeur on a vast scale – he wrote scarcely a single note of music in this period. In the crucial year of 1848 he turned his attention to various dramatic projects linked in some way or another with current revolutionary ideas (admittedly, violence did not flare on the streets of Dresden in that year, but the points were indeed set for the violence to come). Wagner's writing at this time shows a growing tendency away from history towards myth: *Lohengrin* certainly had a historical background – the Hungarian invasion from the East, and the arrival of the German Emperor to rally the nobles of Brabant – as would his ambitious planned work *Friedrich I*, a play in five acts at which he worked during the winter of 1848–9 (some sketches exist dating from 1846). There is no music, for this was intended as a spoken play dealing with the struggle between two warring factions, the Ghibellines (led by Friedrich Barbarossa) and the Guelphs (the Duke of Saxony and Henry the Lion). It was to have been written in the popular rhymed verse of the Middle High German epic poets. Only a draft was completed, as Wagner soon realized that such a vast topic – dealing with battles, a siege, the capture of Milan, the Diet of Augsburg, humiliation and banishment, court festivities at Mainz, peace with the Lombards, reconciliation with the Pope, news of the fall of Jerusalem and the departure for the Holy Land – far exceeded the limits of traditional theatre. But he also left it merely as a draft because he was increasingly convinced that political history was an unsuitable subject for music drama and that myth alone could fill this gap (this, in all probability, was why he abandoned his projected *Die Sarazenin*, an opera in five acts dating from 1841). He turned his attention to an essay, 'Die Wibelungen. Weltgeschichte aus der Legende' (The Wibelungs: World History in Legend). Regarding the 'Wibelungen' name: Wagner took remarkable liberties in implying that the Waiblinger, also known as the Ghibellines, would give their name to the Nibelungen. The hoard becomes a symbol of world power with Friedrich Barbarossa ruling with his mightly sword. The essay ends with the cry: 'When will you return, Friedrich, you glorious Siegfried! and strike the evil, gnawing dragon?'[8] This can be seen as Wagner's last attempt to merge history and myth; it is the first extended reference to the Nibelungs, to a hoard of gold and a glorious hero. And Barbarossa ultimately yields to Siegfried, the mystical embodiment of the true man, glorious in his heroism.

The legends of the Nibelungs now proved irresistible to Wagner and in the summer and autumn of 1848 he sketched out his own version of the saga as *Die Nibelungen-Saga (Mythos)*. He completed this on 4 October and would later publish it with the qualifying subheading 'Sketch for a Drama'. For the time being, only the last and most fully developed section was turned into an opera libretto, *Siegfrieds Tod* (Siegfried's Death), the forerunner of *Götterdämmerung* (1874), in November of the same year. In December Wagner read, as would become increasingly his wont, the completed *Siegfrieds Tod* to friends invited to his house, including Gottfried Semper, the future architect, also Hans von Bülow, later to become the cuckolded husband of Cosima d'Agoult, daughter of Franz Liszt. The gods, Wagner explained, must perish to allow the truly human to triumph. After this, surprisingly perhaps, he would steep himself in the gospels and Hegel's philosophy of history.

The study of the gospels bore fruit: from early 1849 there dates another detailed sketch, this time for a five act play entitled *Jesus von Nazareth* (parts also date from 1846). In *Eine Mitteilung an meine Freunde* (VI, pp. 311–12) Wagner will explain what drew him to the figure of Christ: disenchantment with public affairs and feeling more and more isolated from the world in which he found himself he was increasingly attracted by Christ as fellow-sufferer and soulmate. Wagner identifies Christ's rejection of the corrupt Roman world with his own disgust of, and rebellion against, contemporary life. Much is heard in Wagner's sketch of the conflict between Love and Law: Love is the Law of life, but man has created Law to limit life in order to protect the three pillars of society: power, property and marriage. Free love, Jesus/Wagner seems to believe, can only realize itself outside the Law, even against the law, and these revolutionary ideas will later emerge in the *Ring*. Bakunin, so Wagner tells us, chose not to be present at the reading of *Jesus von Nazareth* but simply recommended, in true anarchist fashion, that, if any music *were* written the tenor sing 'chop his head off!', the soprano 'hang him!' and the bass 'Fire! Fire!'[9] Jesus as revolutionary? But violence was anathema to Jesus and, according to Wagner, he could not support an uprising against Rome planned by Judas and Barrabas but longed, ultimately, for death.

Meanwhile the political situation in Saxony grew increasingly more tense; in May Wagner wrote his poem 'Die Not' (Need – or Tribulation) which prophesied a 'holy incendiary' against the cities of Mammon and the return of man and nature to a state of paradise (v, pp. 267–70). For what was to be his last Palm Sunday concert Wagner rehearsed Beethoven's Ninth Symphony, at the end of which Bakunin called to Wagner that if all the world's music were to go up in flames at the coming world conflagration he would fight to the death to defend *this* work. Wagner now took no pains to conceal his involvement in the revolution that was surely coming; his rhapsodic essay 'Die Revolution' appeared in the *Volksblätter* and personified revolution as an angel of destruction, as a storm about to purify the world, bringing a new gospel of joy: 'I shall destroy the power of the mighty, of property . . . Only a free man is holy; nothing is higher than he' (v, p. 238). Three weeks later Friedrich August II dissolved the chambers and abrogated the constitution. Röckel fled to Prague and Wagner took over responsibilities for his journal; rumour circulated that the Saxon king had called for Prussian troops to help put down the impending uprising. On 3 May troops fired on the populace and barricades were ostensibly erected under Semper's supervision.

Many wild rumours have circulated concerning Wagner's activities during these heady days. It is certain that he used the *Volksblätter* printing presses to circulate flyers ('Are you with us against foreign troops?') which he distributed among Saxon soldiers during a ceasefire, but it has not been proved that he assisted in making hand grenades. We know that Wilhelmine Schröder-Devrient, from her bay window, spurned on the armed insurgents and that Wagner in the lull before the storm, walking about the barricades, brooded on a drama, *Achilleus*, the theme of which had occupied him for some time. We have stressed that from the earliest years he had been fascinated by classical Greek tragedy; this had been quickened by a performance of Gluck's *Iphigenie in Aulis* he had organized in 1846, and by a reading of Euripides and, above all, Aeschylus. *My Life* tells of the effect that the *Agamemnon* had had upon him, the state of rapture that the play had evoked (and famous would be the reading of the *Oresteia* which he would arrange over three nights in Wahnfried in 1880).[10] Now in May 1849 he saw Achilles as a Greek counterpart to Siegfried, half human and half divine; Achilles would reject this immortality which his mother Thetis offers him, for man is greater than the gods, or, rather, he is a perfection of god: 'Der Mensch ist die Vervollkommnung des Gottes' (III, p. 273). There is much of Feuerbach's anthropomorphism here, but the sketch remained a fragment (yet Wagner would not neglect to mention it in a letter to King Ludwig in 1865). In the febrile turmoil of his mind it would seem that Siegfried, Jesus and Achilles represented embodiments of God-turned-man; almost simultaneously he was contemplating three mythologies: Germanic, biblical and Greek. But his unerring instinct told him that there was only one true path for him, a path adumbrated by the *Nibelungenmythos*, a path that would be long and arduous but that would lead to triumph and world renown in 1876.

On 4 May the king fled the city and on the following night Wagner watched from the tower of the Kreuzkirche to report on any Prussian troop movements: he whiled away the nocturnal hours in deep speculation with a teacher called Herr Berthold. Prussian troops entered the city and bombarded it; the opera house went up in flames (Wagner would be later maligned and erroneously held responsible for this). The uprising was swiftly crushed and Wagner fled with his wife to Chemnitz. Röckel was not so lucky: he was captured and initially sentenced to death. On 16 May a warrant for Wagner's arrest was displayed in Dresden: he was now officially on the wanted list and was, ostensibly, a

Barricades in Dresden in 1849, the closing act of the Europe-wide revolutions that erupted in 1848.

dangerous radical. Liszt advised him to flee Germany and get, if he could, to Paris, where he would be safe; with a forged passport Wagner crossed into Switzerland via Lake Constance and Rorschach and made his way to Zurich. His first act here was to read to a small group of acquaintances his *Siegfrieds Tod*. He would not step upon German soil again until 1860, nor write a note of music for the massive work germinating inside him until November 1865.

Before looking, briefly, at Wagner's *Reformschriften* it might be appropriate to mention Wagner's own 'Zukunftsmusik' (Music of the Future, 1860), a 'succinct, attractively written and comparatively balanced account' of his artistic standpoint.[11] He settled in Paris in 1859 to bring about the new production of *Tannhäuser* and took the advice of a French friend, Frédéric Villot, to dispel the impression that he was somehow a megalomaniac desirous of imposing so-called 'Music of the Future' upon the world. Wagner agreed: he was also arranging translations of *Der fliegende Holländer*, *Tannhäuser*, *Lohengrin* and *Tristan und Isolde* and wrote the open letter to Villot keeping the inverted commas which had been placed around the work by Villot to imply that the term was somehow eccentric (it was published as a brochure in German shortly afterwards).

With remarkable (and unusual) modesty Wagner explains that he had been in an abnormal state of mind when writing the Zurich treatises (the Reformschriften); no artist before him had been so 'sorely beset', dealing with problems that seemed intractable. He had had to work in a field of study (abstract thought) to which he was unaccustomed; now, surprisingly perhaps, he does not wish to rehearse his earlier argument, sparing his readers the details of *Kunst und Revolution* (Art and Revolution), let alone the minutely detailed expositions of *Oper und Drama*, which he now sees must have been of far greater interest to him than it ever would be to others, now or in the future. Is he being disingenuous? It is obvious that he is trying to popularize his work among the French and plays down the theoretical writings; he is neither vainglorious nor insisting on blind obedience. And although he himself would modify his earlier statements and even ignored the tenets proposed when artistic creativity returned to him, there is much fascinating material in the *Reformschriften* which we ignore at our peril.

It has been argued that Wagner's flight as a political fugitive came just at the right time: that he was ready in 1848–9 to make a clean break with the past, artistically, politically and emotionally.[12] A thorough stocktaking was needed, a reassessment of his life and his artistic aims. He knew that he had to express the psychology and the emotions of his characters far more deeply than in conventional opera and felt the need more and more to concentrate on the spoken word, or the dialogue. He even contemplated doing away with music altogether and concentrating on spoken drama but fortunately this extreme position did not last: it was the synthesis of music and drama for which he strove, the need to rid opera of specious frivolities and meretricious ostentation. Opera, he felt, had become relegated to mere entertainment for the jaded bourgeoisie in a world of money-grubbing capitalism. He saw himself increasingly as a German composer destined to follow the difficult yet sublime path leading from Beethoven. The blandishments of the French and Italians were to be superseded by something far more noble, far more powerful. Beethoven had shown the way by the triumphant fusion of poetry and music in the last movement of the Ninth Symphony, and Wagner's dream of the artwork of the future, *his* artwork, was the only possible creative step, channelling into the bed of music drama the great stream that Beethoven had sent pouring into German music.

Some two months after arriving in Zurich, in July 1849, Wagner wrote his penetrating essay *Die Kunst und die Revolution*: his two main targets were Christianity and capitalism. in In its rejection of sensuality and sexual fulfilment, Christianity, Wagner argues, is necessarily inimitable to art, which joyfully praises life in all its tragic glory (his later disciple Friedrich Nietzsche would later learn much from him here). The Greek world was a place where men gathered to exult in this commonly felt mythology; here art was the greatest and most aweful manifestation of life. Greek tragedy, Wagner argues, represented the culmination of the human spirit; modern art, in contrast, is a mere chaos of hollow impressions jostling without rhyme or reason. There were indeed great masters – Shakespeare, a second Caesar, who opened up the infinite realm of human nature, and Beethoven, who carried music to heights hitherto unheard of. But these are ignored by the rapacious rabble who only seek money and self-gratification; there is no longer any great art but trash peddled by contemporary opera houses and theatres. Art, for the Greeks, was the highest expression of activity in a race that had developed its physical beauty in union with itself and with nature. Wagner here slates the cultured decadence of his age and, in a very Romantic fashion, elevates the Greek ideal above all else.

A combined artwork is then extolled: a *Gesamtkunstwerk* in which the separate arts of poetry, music and dance are fused, and a people, a *Volk*, finds itself reflected and transfigured. This was a utopian vision indeed, and one to which Wagner would not necessarily adhere, but it was very much in his mind at this time. Indeed, when fused with various revolutionary ideas, it contributed in a certain sense to the genesis of *Siegfrieds Tod*. Egoism can only, it seems, be overcome by an idea very close to communism, a fusion of the individual with the people. Heady days indeed for this German musician on the run; days interrupted, however, by the arrival of his wife (much aged) with dog and parrot.

On 4 November Wagner completed the more substantial essay 'Das Kunstwerk der Zukunft' (The Artwork of the Future), which was dedicated to Feuerbach. In this essay the ideas put forward in the earlier pamphlet were expanded and elaborated, and an increasingly tendentious tone becomes apparent. The *Volk* is idealized in a manner derived from Herder and Rousseau; the various art forms (music, poetry and dance) are surveyed and their separate developments are lamented. Wagner believed that they had lost a synthesis that once had existed. Some twenty years before Nietzsche's invocation of Dionysian bacchantes and their expressive dancing, Wagner praises not only music and drama but Terpsichore, the muse of dance. But the noble art of dance became mere meretricious titillation, an empty charade, an absurdity: 'glorious dance' became 'wretched dance' (VI, p. 51). It may be strange to think of Wagner waxing enthusiastic for dance; it should be remembered, however, that he took a keen interest in expressive movement in the Parisian bacchanal and insisted that a maître de ballet from Dessau, Richard Fricke, advise on the movement of the Rhinemaidens in *Das Rheingold*. Isadora Duncan would also later dance in Bayreuth. 'Das Kunstwerk der Zukunft' also contained the famous description of Beethoven's Seventh Symphony as 'the apotheosis of the dance' (VI, p. 66). What is needed, Wagner unashamedly argues, is an 'artwork of the future' based on the Greek example: this is what the musical dramatist (and we know his name) is working towards. Beethoven had pointed the way to this (Wagnerian) idea, and the fourth section of Part Two of the tract glorifies him, his Seventh Symphony and his Ninth, triumphant in the musico-dramatic climax: 'Be embraced, ye millions! This kiss is for the whole of mankind!' (VI, p. 68).

Extravagant claims indeed. This publication by Wagner may be censured for its inaccuracies and transparent self-serving tendentiousness. But the emphasis on *emotion*, on mythical awareness and intense subjectivity, will strike deep chords. What Wagner is envisioning is the expression of intense emotion that will take the audience by storm; Wagner inveighs in this tract against abstract reason, against *Wissenschaft*, which threatens to dominate life. If conscious, autocratic thought could dominate life fully, if it could usurp the vital impulse and divert it to some other purpose than the claims of life themselves, then, Wagner writes, Life itself would be dethroned and swallowed up in Science. 'And truly, Science, in her overweening arrogance has dreamed of such a triumph – as witness our tight-reigned state and our modern art: the sexless, barren children of this dream' (VI, p. 13). Intense emotion, then, but there is also here an insistence on the spoken word: continuous musical accompaniment must never drown, but enhance the elements of speech – this Wagner the theoretician insists. The gap between theory and practice would be wide indeed, as our impassioned idealist would learn, yet his exaggeration and sweeping generalizations, the torrential volubility and supreme self-confidence, are extremely engaging.

'Das Kunstwerk der Zukunft' ends, curiously perhaps, with ecstatic exhortation to the Germans from another of Wagner's projects, one, in fact, which came close to fruition: *Wieland der Schmied* (Wieland the Smith). The material concerning Wieland (known in English as Wayland) fascinated Wagner, and he worked on the project from December 1849 to March 1850. As always his choice of subject-matter sprang from a deep personal involvement in the story of the mythical smith who is held in bondage by a cruel king, then finally manages to forge himself wings and flies away to freedom with the swan-maiden Schwanhilde. There are some striking parallels between Wieland and the Nibelungen material, and it has been claimed that Wagner's interest in the smith even competed with his interest in Siegfried for a while. There is in *Wieland* a ring which gives power; the forging of a powerful sword; a Hagen-like figure (Gram). Bathilde is a strange fusion of Ortrud and Brünnhilde; there is a wounded swan (to be found later, admittedly, in *Parsifal*) and the removal of Schwanhilde's wings, which enables Wieland to 'recognize with delight a beautiful female form' (as in *Siegfried*). Both works, Wagner felt, were genuine folk legends, and the people who brought forth such wonders were to be praised. 'Oh unique, glorious people! *This* is what you have created – *you* are this Wieland! Forge your wings, and rise upwards!' (VI, p. 157)

As is becoming apparent, Wagner was writing feverishly at this time, not music but prose – tracts, essays, pamphlets and sketches. His wife, appalled, wondered how they were going to live and constantly reprimanded him for having lost his prestigious post and becoming involved with cranks, anarchists and revolutionaries. He was fortunate enough to meet Julie Ritter, widow of a merchant, who had settled in Dresden after her mother's death and became a friend and benefactor. In 1850 Julie Ritter offered Wagner an annual allocation of 500 Talers, which she would generously continue to pay until late 1854, despite the ignominious Bordeaux affair with Jessie Laussot. This lady, née Taylor, was the wife of a wine merchant and, overwhelmed by Wagner's music and ideas – she had, purely by chance, been present at the first performance of *Tannhäuser* – had offered him an annual allowance of 2,500 francs. The munificence of these two ladies had kept the Wagners afloat and, encouraged rather rashly by Liszt, Wagner agreed to try once more to take Paris by storm, this time with *Wieland*. Paris . . . However much he railed against this 'kept woman' he was still fascinated by her and above all by her Opéra, which, dominated by Meyerbeer, had demonstrated to the world with incomparable splendour, sophistication and technical wizardry how the grandest of grand effects could be achieved. Before settling in Zurich he had spent some weeks in Paris (May and June 1849) meeting emigrés like Gottfried Semper and Wilhelm Heinse; he had also, by chance, come across Meyerbeer at the publisher Schlesingers; Meyerbeer flippantly asked him if he were writing scores for the barricades. Disgusted, he had written to Liszt asking for the fare back to Switzerland, where he held forth again against the wretchedness of the cultural scene in Paris. He returned to this intriguing city in February 1850 and, on 20 February, steeled himself to see Meyerbeer's *Le prophète*, that opera which had surpassed even the enormous successes of *Robert le diable* and *Les Huguenots* and which had broken all records, having earned the management of the opera house more than 10,000 francs on one evening. The premiere of *Le prophète* on 16 April had brought expectation to fever pitch (the French parliament did not meet that evening as the deputies had taken over the grand tier and the boxes) and the audience was not disappointed: this was generally believed to have been the opera of the century, and an embittered German in the stalls would later write in his memoirs of his chagrin at having had to see it, his rage at the work's shallowness and his determination to ignore the whole thing completely.[13]

But *My Life*, written years later, is notoriously tendentious, and certain letters of 1850 imply that his experience of seeing *Le prophète* was more differentiated, more complex.[14] A brief description of the opera must suffice. Meyerbeer had insisted that the tone be '*sombre et fanatique*', and it portrays the events leading up to the seizure of Münster by the Anabaptists in 1535 and the ensuing catastrophe. There is nothing urbane about the opera, no gorgeous costumes, no ballroom scene. The settings were based on Dutch landscape paintings; there is also a typical Dutch tavern scene in Act Two where we meet Jean van Leyden and his mother Fides. It is he who will claim that he is the Son of God, with apocalyptic consequences. Most famous was Act Three, with its memorable skating ballet. Paris had never experienced such a thing – no grand ballroom but a wintry setting near Münster. However, the skilful use of perspective during the ballet (on skilfully concealed roller-skates) caused a sensation, as did the triumphant call to arms by Jean van Leyden; the dawn broke, and the sun rose over the town of Münster, the New Jerusalem. (The effect of the sunrise was indeed remarkable: an arc lamp whose intensity could be regulated was used for the first time on the operatic stage.) Act

Four contained the magnificent coronation of Jean van Leyden as the Son of God in the cathedral of Münster; here Meyerbeer achieved a monumental effect with an organ, children's choruses and massed choirs in eight sections positioned on different levels. The climax is the interruption of the service by Fides recognizing the crowned prophet as her son, and this son's denial of his mother. The final act begins in a vast underground vault in the palace at Münster where Fides is imprisoned and sings her famous aria (which Wagner claims to have detested). The scene finally changes to a festive banquet, but at its height the imperial soldiers burst in to reclaim the city. The tower serving as a powder magazine explodes, bringing the roof down with it; the palace is engulfed in flames; the Anabaptists sing that Hell awaits them and Jean van Leyden, the false prophet, dies in the arms of his mother.

The effect of this immense opera was shattering: Meyerbeer was praised to the skies and overwhelmed with honours, including a golden laurel leaf. He was made a member of the Légion d'honneur and received 19,000 francs for his work, the highest sum that the Paris Opéra had ever bestowed. And Wagner?

Letters to Theodor Uhlig, a German violinist, music critic and composer (also illegitimate son of Friedrich August II of Saxony), are enlightening here; the first, written within days of Wagner's having seen the work, refers to its undesirable impact and the tumultuous applause;[15] the second (13 March) refers to the 'prophet of the new world' (Meyerbeer) and describes the experience of having seen the work as a revelation ('*Offenbarung*').[16] The noble, the truthful, the pure and the divinely human, he writes, can still, it seems, be experienced 'fervently' in the present. But a note of irony is unmistakable here, for it is these ideals which Wagner was seeking to express in *his* works, *his* music dramas, dramas as yet unwritten or unperformed. And Wagner knew that only Paris could bring forth such works under ideal circumstances with the remarkable resources that were available there.[17] It was a bitter pill for him to swallow: *Wieland der Schmied* was utterly inappropriate, and the new path that he was determined to follow, from history to myth, hardly seemed feasible. And he had to accept the fact that whereas *Lohengrin* had still not been performed, *Le prophète* was going from strength to strength (in 1850 alone, it would be staged in 30 opera houses in Europe and America.)

It is not an exaggeration to claim that Wagner underwent an existential crisis in the spring of 1850, consumed as he was by envy and uncertainty about his own musical direction: the future seemed bleak and uncertain, the Nibelungen material shapeless and inchoate; the Parisians had treated him with supercilious indifference; his wife scarcely understood what he was saying or doing. On 24 March he gratefully accepted an invitation from the Laussot family to visit their home in Bordeaux. The 23-year-old Jessie felt pity for Wagner, and this pity soon turned to infatuation. Wagner showed her the *Wieland* manuscript and Jessie saw herself as the swan-maiden Schwanhilde (her piano playing was good but her singing betrayed a hysterical tone which should have warned him).[18] Each confided in the other that their marriages were unhappy. Wagner had tired of the endless recriminations from Minna; she now insisted on using the formal 'Sie' form when writing to him. He explained to Jessie that he had had enough and would flee to Greece and the near East; Jessie, as Schwanhilde, would flee with him. Exhilarated, yet also confused, Wagner returned to Paris on 5 April and sought solace in the score of *Lohengrin*, pondering on possible theatres where it might be performed. A letter from Jessie explained that she was determined to leave her husband and join him; he considered the possibility of sailing from Marseilles to Malta, then eastwards. But news came that Jessie had confided in her mother, who had immediately informed Eugène Laussot, who now threatened to kill Wagner. This farcical episode ended with a letter from Jessie regretting the whole incident and Wagner being expelled from Bordeaux by the police.

To clear his mind of the whole absurd farce Wagner undertook a strenuous walking tour with Julie Ritter's son Karl through Switzerland to Zermatt and the foot of the Matterhorn, finally returning to Zurich, and Minna, on 3 July.

Wagner's state of disorientation after the shock of experiencing 'the new prophet' in Paris may have contributed to these extramarital confusions; what *is* highly likely is that the notorious twenty-page article 'Das Judentum in der Musik' (Jewishness in Music) which he published in the *Neue Zeitschrift für Musik* under the pseudonym 'K. Freigedank' is a direct result of smarting under Meyerbeer's success and lashing out in response. (In 1869 he would later reprint the discussion as an independent pamphlet under his own name, to the consternation of many of his admirers.) His friend Uhlig had used the expression '*hebräischer Kunstgeschmack*' (Jewish artistic taste) in an attempt to underpin his conviction that Meyerbeer must be inferior and to imply that a 'good Christian' would find his work forced, exaggerated, unnatural and over-sophisticated.[19] Robert Schumann had also spoken disparagingly of Meyerbeer; he had, however, praised Mendelssohn's oratorio *Paulus* and Uhlig had found this inconsistent, implying that both composers were somehow inadequate. Wagner now felt the need to jump into the fray with both fists flying and support Uhlig. Henceforth he would be seen by many as a rabid anti-Semite, or even as preparing the way for the Holocaust.

We must now look coolly at his pamphlet to see what it actually *says*. He has most certainly been stung by Meyerbeer's success and feels bitter against those with wealth and influence who manipulated the operatic world in Paris: many were Jews. But 'Das Judentum in der Musik' is not a crude anti-Semitic rant, despite the offensive comments on the cacophonous nature of Jewish speech and the disagreeably foreign nature of the Jew; if Wagner is to be stereotyped as an anti-Semite it must be made clear that this anti-Semitism is of a very idiosyncratic kind.

His central argument is that the truly creative artist is necessarily rooted in a society and expresses its preoccupations, needs and desires. He has absorbed these from his earliest childhood and is enmeshed in this society. He is part of his *Volk* and is aware of their myths and legends without being conscious of it. For Jewish artists this is impossible, for they have only recently (after the French Revolution) been freed from the ghetto and are only just being assimilated into European society. The Jewish composers of Wagner's day were the first emancipated Jews, often speaking German with a foreign accent. They may have been desirous of writing German music to compare with that of the greatest (Beethoven), but Wagner believed they could never do this: they had turned their backs on their Hebrew past but could never be 'the conscious and proclaimed unconscious' of the German people which Wagner believed all art to be.[20] The Jew could only seek to emulate, to succeed, but his gifts would be sterile and shallow. Mendelssohn, Wagner tells us, had many talents as a musician, much refinement of taste and the utmost integrity, but could never produce that deep, shattering, searing effect that we expect from great music. In 1879, in his essay 'Über das Dichten und Komponieren' (On Writing and Composing) (IX, p. 294), Mendelssohn's *Hebrides* overture is publicly praised by Wagner as 'one of the most beautiful pieces of music that we have'; Mendelssohn excels, then, as a landscape painter, not a communicator of profound emotion (yet do we not hear echoes of *Die schöne Melusine* at the opening of *Das Rheingold*?). Guarded praise, then, but none for a 'Jewish composer of our time, lauded far and wide'. This composer knows how to manipulate and dazzle; he appeals to the blasé and the wealthy and provides them with meretricious spectacle. He wishes to create genuine works of art, but cannot. His name is never mentioned but Wagner's readers would certainly know that it was Giacomo Meyerbeer, originally Jakob Liebmann Beer. The Jewish celebrity, Wagner believes, was typical of a bungled assimilation into a corrupt civilization alienated from true art; it is only the artwork of the future, we infer, that could transcend this.

The last two paragraphs of Wagner's essay have given rise to enormous discussion and grotesque claims that he is somehow pleading for the physical annihilation of the Jews in his use of the world '*Untergang*' (meaning sinking, decline, ruin or destruction). Great care must be taken to understand what he means, for the essay moves finally into realms that are difficult of access. He reminds his readers of the writer Ludwig Börne (born Juda Löw Baruch) who had died in Paris in 1837. Börne had converted to Christianity but, Wagner explains, he failed to find redemption among us (the Germans) and was forced to realize that he would only do so when *we ourselves were redeemed as true human beings*' (Wagner's italics).[21] This redemption, or self-annihilation, is necessary, Wagner explains, and the whole of mankind must submit to it if we are to overcome our alienation from our true humanity. The Jews are invited not merely to assimilate but to 'join us unreservedly in this work, the work of redemption . . . and we shall be united and indivisible!'

These diffuse and wildly utopian aspirations need not give rise to offence, but Wagner added a last line, an exhortation to the Jews: 'But remember one thing alone can redeem you from a curse which weighs upon you: the redemption of Ahasuerus – destruction!'[22] We have met Ahasuerus in our discussion of *Der fliegende Holländer*: he finds salvation after the curse of existence is lifted from him by love. Both Gentile *and* Jew, Wagner attempts to explain, must die to the modern world with its greed and rapacity and seek to become reborn. There are remarkable similarities here with Karl Marx, who had written in his essay 'Zur Judenfrage' (On the Jewish Question, 1843) of the need for the Jewish spirit, which means blatant materialism, to be abolished; the emancipation of the Jew, Marx had written, can only be achieved by the emancipation of humanity from Judaism. Wagner goes one further: 'the Jewish question cannot be solved by integrating the Jews into existing society, but only by "abolishing" Judaism as part of a more general process involving the need to overcome man's alienation from self, which in itself is the result of the domination of capital.'[23] To claim, then, that Wagner preaches the physical annihilation of the Jewish race is preposterous: mankind as a whole must 'die' to the modern world and its materialism to become reborn. It is indeed tempting to know whether or not Wagner knew or had seen Salomon Mosenthal's play *Deborah*, written in Vienna in 1849, in whose fourth act the messianic hour is awaited when both Christian and Jew all become – human beings ('Menschen').

A work must be written, Wagner knows, to show the emergence of a new world, a new man and a new society, for the old world, with its greed and its lust for power, must be destroyed. *Lohengrin*, we know, had been performed on 28 August 1850 in Weimar; now, however, Wagner was restless and brooding on a new venture, a new vision. The idea of a festival theatre (since Paris is beyond consideration now) emerges in a letter to Kietz on 14 September 1850.[24] If he had 10,000 thalers, Wagner writes, he would build a wooden theatre where *Siegfrieds Tod* would be performed three times a week, after which the theatre would be dismantled. Replying to Uhlig, who had recommended a '*Wasser-cur*' (hydrotherapy) for various ailments, Wagner replied on 22 October that it is not a '*Wasser-cur*' but a '*Feuer-cur*', purification by fire, that is needed.[25] He continues that 'in all level-headedness' that he no longer believes in any revolution save the one which begins with the incineration of Paris: fire will cleanse all. But he is now on the point of finishing his major theoretical work, *Oper und Drama*, the original draft of which he will complete in January 1851.

Why was another theoretical discussion needed? It was a theoretical counterpart to the *Ring* drama that was maturing within him: 'Das Kunstwerk der Zukunft' was, perhaps, too general a blueprint and Wagner felt the need for a more detailed justification for these new, revolutionary projects. An article in volume IV of *Die Gegenwart* (The Present) appearing in Leipzig in 1850 may have been the catalyst.[26] An anonymous contributor argued that Germany possessed a 'Meister' who had totally understood the future as promised by Meyerbeer's operas. This 'Meister' was one Richard Wagner, who had attempted to adapt Meyerbeer's great achievement for the German stage. But his, Wagner's, genius had not yet been clarified, for Wagner was trapped in inner contradictions and did not possess the architectonic skills which Meyerbeer could muster in his powerful dramas. Wagner's operas, our critic concludes, have not yet become part of the staple diet of the German stage because he has not yet electrified the general public by 'granting those concessions which are allowed in Meyerbeer's work'. If another excuse were needed after 'Das Judentum in der Musik' to lash out at Meyerbeer then this article certainly provided it and Wagner's belligerence knew no bounds. (The writer's view that it was Mendelssohn who might point the way in which opera could develop, Wagner passed over in irritation, not fury.) He would utterly repudiate any indebtedness to Meyerbeer and show an ignorant public what the *Gesamtkunstwerk* was; the likes of Meyerbeer would be consigned to outer darkness.

Oper und Drama, this very substantial thesis of some 100,000 words, is indebted to Feuerbach's praise of the senses and to the Romantic cult of emotion: the *Gesamtkunstwerk*, the artwork of the future, would communicate via the senses and exclusively to the emotions.[27] We become knowing, Wagner insists, via feeling. Music is the language of emotion par excellence, but verse must likewise play a part in the word-tone synthesis and communicate fervently and intensively. Great importance is given to alliteration, concentration and free rhythm, which are suited, Wagner claims, to express that which is primitive, fundamental and basic (see below). Most striking are Wagner's meditations on myth. The unique thing about myth, he writes, is that it is true for all time and that its content, condensed to the utmost intensity, is inexhaustible for all time. Song, Wagner writes, is the beginning and the end of language as feeling is the beginning and the end of understanding and myth the beginning and the end of history (vii, p. 218). Getting into his stride, Wagner also writes that music is a woman; her nature is love and she only receives full individuality at the moment of abandonment (vii, p. 114). Her task is to bring forth in joy and fulfilment that which she has conceived. Who is the man who can earn such love so utterly? 'Let us consider well before we sacrifice the love of this woman whether the man's reciprocating love is servile or something necessary and redemptive: let us look closely at – the poet!' (vii, p. 118). Wagner now hammers home the point that the woman (music) receives a soul from the man, the poet; he goes on to compare Italian opera with the prostitute, French opera with the coquette and German opera (until, we assume, his own arrival) with the prude. But now the interaction of word and music, of poet and musician, can bring forth true greatness: it is not the sensuality of the prostitute, nor the frivolity of the coquette, but deep and genuine love which brings forth the artwork of the future. The poetic vision is the productive seed which bestows upon woman, in Wagner's metaphoric scheme, the life that she will bear. It is, in short, the total work of art, the *Gesamtkunstwerk*, which will emerge as a redemptive experience that will show to the world what a rebirth of myth, suffused with music of the utmost intensity, can achieve and offer to an astonished world; the nadir of the contemporary operatic world – music by Meyerbeer, libretto by Scribe, the vacuous presentation of shallow 'effects without causes' (vii, p. 98) – will be banished forever.

Wagner's metaphors are frequently striking and another associates music with the traveller across the seas, and poetry with the traveller across the land. Musician and poet go their different ways in opposite directions, meeting again on the other side of the planet. The poet describes plains, valleys, mountains and the world of men; the musician describes the wonders of the ocean, the storms and tempests, the terrors of the deep and the strange-shaped monsters which fill him half with terror, half with joy. *He* has seen more wondrous things and the poet now climbs on the musician's boat, rejoicing in the giant-bolted framework of the ship and in the billows rising proudly before them (VII, pp. 293–5). The ship, Wagner tells us, is the orchestra, and the poet now marvels at the oceanic mysteries which this orchestra enables him to experience. In short, music is portrayed as the female element which is fructified by the *word*; it is also described as an oceanic, primeval element on which the poet sets sail. The word, it seems, is like a golden light which breaks into the waters: the prelude to *Das Rheingold*, the 164 bars of E flat major of a world in the depths of the Rhine, with the light gleaming in the darkness, is perhaps adumbrated here, the classical features of a creation myth.

Two other important discussions in *Oper und Drama*, this fecund and fascinating cornucopia, concern *Stabreim* and what would later be known as leitmotifs, motifs of presentiment and reminiscence. One of the hallmarks of the *Ring* and one which could be (and was) easily mocked by critics and opponents is the use of *Stabreim*, or alliterative verse. We know that Wagner steeped himself in a study of Old and Middle High German literature and that his debt to scholars such as Ettmüller, Simrock and von der Hagen is considerable. He was personally indebted to Ettmüller as translator of the Icelandic Eddas, also the *Nibelungenlied* (he knew Ettmüller personally during his Swiss years). Alliterative verse is ubiquitous in the old Germanic poetry: lines consist of a consistent number of metrically stressed syllables and a variable number of unstressed; these lines fall into two parts and the linking element is alliteration, indicating that this was poetry and not prose. Wagner seized on this, claiming that end rhymes were otiose and that *Stabreim* was superior in its emotional impact. His belief, however, that '*stabgereimter Vers*' was more genuine because it derived from the *Volk* is certainly spurious, but it certainly can link concepts from different sensual spheres ('weal' and 'woe', for example) as a composer modulates from one key to another expressing joy and pain; text and music are thus fused together more effortlessly. Alliterative verse is not mere affectation in the *Ring* but is of its essence, and Wagner would most certainly have been delighted to learn that recent scholarship has suggested that all Germanic verse was originally sung in a form of free, recitative cantillation.[28]

The second important discussion concerns leitmotifs (although Wagner himself never used this term). These are not merely 'visiting cards' (*pace* Debussy): they are a device to bind together and tighten the structure of the musical drama. Wagner is arguing that music cannot think but it *can* materialize thoughts, making known their emotional content, and the essential nature of his music, its phenomenal power of compressing into a few bars the most profound emotional and psychological situations, is helped beyond doubt by the orchestra's use of motifs which remind, hint, yearn, threaten and foretell. These motifs frequently act as the subconscious mind of the protagonist and enrich immeasurably that which the listener experiences. They have been called 'musical ideas',[29] accumulating additional layers of significance through their modified reappearance. Wagner was obviously not the first to use reminiscence motifs. He certainly found them in Weber (and to a lesser extent in Spohr and E.T.A. Hoffmann) but his skilful manipulation of *Grundthemen* will endow his work with an intensely dramatic impulse rarely equalled.

To conclude, we recall that Wagner explained, in his open letter to Villot of 1860, that he was in an abnormal state of mind when writing his theoretical works and that he would spare his French readers the details of *Oper und Drama*, which may have interested him when he wrote it but not many others. There is an undeniable disingenuousness in 'Zukunftsmusik's self-deprecation: the *Reform-schriften* show no signs of abnormality but had to be written and contain many valid and stimulating insights. In *Oper und Drama* we must bear in mind that Wagner was giving us a blueprint for works as yet unwritten, and during the composition of these works he would not adhere slavishly to any rigid scheme. The completion of *Der Ring des Nibelungen* would be a lifetime's work, after all, and it was interrupted by two towering masterpieces, *Tristan und Isolde* and *Die Meistersinger von Nürnberg*. Wagner's earlier ideas on man and society, on life and death, would be profoundly altered by a reading of the philosopher Schopenhauer, as we shall see in the next chapter; Wagner would develop quite naturally and not adhere to earlier stipulations (the 'Beethoven' essay of 1870, for example, extols the primacy of music above all other arts). A foolish consistency may well be the hobgoblin of little minds, as Emerson once wrote; Wagner's mind was certainly not one of these.

4

Exploration and Consolidation

I don't write operas any more . . . I shall call them dramas.

Those friends who managed to finish Wagner's remarkable apologia of 1851 would read the following:

> I intend to perform my work as three independent dramas with a substantial prelude; they will be performed in a dedicated Festival . . . The purpose of this Festival will be realized if I succeed in communicating with my audience, to all of those who have come to understand my intentions not in an intellectual, but in an *emotional* manner. Whatever else is a matter of complete indifference to me.
>
> Very well then: I am giving you enough time and ease to think about all of this – for you will only see me again *when my work is complete*! (VI, p. 325)

So ends, on a note of supreme confidence, the communication to his friends; to those, he insists, who loved him, which he sent out into the world after *Oper und Drama*. Rarely, if ever, has a musician felt the need to compose such an autobiographical retrospective containing bold plans for the future. He dispels the idea that he was a genius; he was, rather, the child in the legend of Queen Wachilde and King Wiking who had been visited by the ill-treated fairy and given that 'ne'er contented mind that ever seeks the new'

(VI, pp. 218, 220). A new artwork, then, a new theatre, a new and vast trilogy and prelude, something never before accomplished. (He would also feel the need to read the whole of *Oper und Drama* to an assembled company in Zurich over twelve separate evenings; the writer Georg Herwegh understandably forewent the experience).

We recall that Wagner drafted the poem *Siegfrieds Tod* three years previously, in November 1848: this was essentially what would later become *Götterdämmerung*. He now, in the summer of 1851, drafted the prose sketch for *Der junge Siegfried* (Young Siegfried), later to become *Siegfried*; not a note of music for any part of the *Ring* would be written until May 1854. The more Wagner grappled with this immense undertaking, the more he realized that he must necessarily push even further back into a mythical past; the prose sketches of what became *Das Rheingold* were written in early November and, immediately afterwards, the prose sketch for *Die Walküre*. Without the remotest idea when the tetralogy would be completed, he nevertheless fervently believed that his new theatre (this time to be built on the banks of the Rhine) would gather an audience who would then understand him, even if at present they were incapable of doing so. A somewhat distraught letter written at the end of 1851 (13 December) talks to Kietz in wild and bloody tones of his hatred of the whole of civilization and a desire to return to nature; men are mere slaves and beneath contempt. In the future, perhaps, the bloodiest and most terrible revolution may come to turn civilized 'wretches' into human beings. He thinks much, he cries, of America (and he would do so again, seriously, as late as 1880). But Beethoven, as always, gave solace: in the winter of 1851–2 Wagner gave three Beethoven concerts, including the music to *Egmont* and the *Coriolanus* overture (the overture to *Tannhäuser* was included). At the gathering at the house of Marschall von Bieberstein, Wagner made the acquaintance of Otto Wesendonck, partner in a New York silk firm, and his 23-year-old wife Mathilde, who had been moved by the Beethoven concerts and was desirous of meeting the conductor. Wagner also conducted four performances of *Der fliegende Holländer* at this time; he worked very carefully with the singers during rehearsals and demonstrated that he was not a mere theorist but very much a man of the theatre (he would publish his comment on performing this work two years later, in 1853).

It is work on the *Ring*, however which of necessity preoccupied him more and more; after finishing the prose sketches of *Das Rheingold* and *Die Walküre* he longed to write music once again. It is remarkable that one of the world's greatest musicians should have lain fallow for such a long period of time, but this music-dramatist was still wrestling in his mind with the possible outcome of the massive tetralogy. Earlier drafts were reworked and the final awareness of Brünnhilde's self-immolation and redemption through death was clarified: the gods would perish and Valhalla be consumed by fire. Since he had drafted the libretti, or poems, in reverse order, Wagner inevitably found that he would have to go back to the versions he had put to paper earlier and redraft them in the light of later developments. On 18 December he read the finished version of *Das Rheingold* and *Die Walküre* to Eliza Wille, a German novelist who had become his confidante, her sister and Herwegh; in 1853 he privately published, in a print run of 50 copies, the completed text of the *Ring* which he would read before invited guests in the now familiar Hotel Baur au Lac; others who had heard of the event also sought entrance. Exhilarated by the success of the readings, and feeling that there was an undeniable *tendresse* developing between himself and Wesendonck's wife Mathilde, Wagner composed for her a sonata with a quote from the current Norn scene of *Götterdämmerung*: 'Wisst Ihr wie das wird?' (Knowst thou what shall be?), a motto that puzzled yet intrigued the recipient.

With Liszt, Wagner undertook a journey to Lake Lucerne. On the Rütli, a place immortalized by Schiller in his *Wilhelm Tell*,

Johann Conrad Dorner's portrait of Mathilde Wesendonck (1850), inspiration for and librettist for the five songs comprising Wagner's *Wesendonck Lieder* (1857).

Wagner, Liszt and Herwegh pledged brotherhood with the famous Rütli oath. Later, Wagner and Herwegh climbed the Julier Pass where Wagner experienced the 'open space on a mountain height' of the second scene of *Das Rheingold*; he would also encounter the 'bless'd desolation on wondrous height' of Act Three of *Siegfried*. But it would be at the end of September, in La Spezia, that Wagner would claim to have had a quasi-mystical experience which was the true impetus and starting point for musical rebirth, the genesis of his *Das Rheingold*; it would be water, not rock, he writes, that would act as the miraculous midwife.[1]

The facts are these. After the walking tour Wagner returned to Zurich dissatisfied and restless; he immersed himself in Goethe's novel *Die Wahlverwandtschaften* (sometimes translated as *Elective Affinities*), a book laced with water, discipline and Romantic dissolution, the static and the fluid, in which the theme of drowning plays a very important part. He took a short trip to Italy (financed by Otto Wesendonck) and travelled to Genoa, where he first saw the Mediterranean, but, ill at ease, he took a boat to La Spezia, where he arrived after a rough sea journey. He took a long walk, then stretched out on the couch in his hotel room and dozed. Then, perhaps, imagination took over: he writes in *My Life* that he fell into the cataleptic state and that from the depth of his conscious mind music arose, the waters of the Rhine where three maidens sported and swam.[2] He felt as though he were sinking into swiftly flowing waters, and a rushing sound formed itself into the E flat major chord which merged into melodic passages of increasing motion and intensity, repeated incessantly in arpeggio formations. He woke in terror, fearing that he were drowning, but then recognized that the orchestral prelude to *Das Rheingold*, which must have been lying dormant within him, had at last been revealed. And now, he claimed, he realized the truth of his own nature: the stream of life was not to flow to him from *without*, but emerge from *within*. But was there more poetry than truth in this account? Why was the experience not related in one or more of his copious letters, nor mentioned at all until the publication of *My Life* in 1873?[3] Be that as it may, Wagner would, some two months later, write down in nine weeks the complete composition sketch of *Das Rheingold*; the E flat major triads and, probably, recollection of the Middle High German 'heilawâc' ('holy water') did their part. And a blueprint had been

An illustration (after a drawing by Knut Ekwall) of the opening scene of *Das Rheingold* (1853–4).

prepared in *Oper und Drama* for the new method of composition: the verse was to be highly alliterative, the language concentrated. The music was to express perfectly the sense of the words, eschewing ensembles and other operatic embellishments. An immensely powerful, dramatic imagination sets the scene, creating images never before envisaged. Wagner had studied, we know, the mystical origin of the Nibelungs, but nowhere in the sources, as Deryck Cooke explains, does a dwarf or any other creature go to the Rhine and meet the Rhine maidens (or Rhine daughters as Wagner calls them) and attempt unsuccessfully to woo them, and then, discovering that the gold they are guarding can be turned into a ring which will bestow world power by renouncing love, then seize it, curse love and flee. This story is Wagner's own.[4]

What the young revolutionary and advocate of free love, disciple of Feuerbach and admirer of much Jung Deutschland writing is telling us is this: any imposition of order upon the natural world, a world harmonic and tranquil, must necessarily lead to suffering.[5] Feuerbach had equated Odin, Wagner's Wotan, with primeval law: that is, contract and constraints. The symbol is the spear, implying that force may be needed to impose his will; this spear he formed by wrenching a branch from the Yggdrasil, the world ash tree of Norse mythology binding heaven, earth and hell. This tree wilted and died, contaminating the forest, which rotted: this the Norns, much later, will tell us in *Götterdämmerung*. Order, then, necessarily brings violation of natural harmony. Wagner implies that civilization brings with it a repression of natural feeling which is incompatible with love. This idea is basic to the *Ring* as a whole. There is much in common between Wotan and Alberich, the former the 'Lichtalberich', ruling by cunning and compromise, the 'wheeler-dealer' of modern parlance; the latter the 'Schwarzalberich', ruling by naked force and violence.[6] Alberich's fellow dwarfs had once lived the lives of carefree craftsmen; now, however, these lives are nothing but toil and hardship. This, as has been pointed out, is skilfully portrayed by the use of leitmotifs: those associated with Wotan's Valhalla are akin to those of the ring forged by Alberich to enable him to become world dictator. *Oper und Drama* expounded at length on the use of the leitmotifs: here we have an immensely rich web of over 100 of them, undergoing subtle modifications and metamorphoses in the orchestra, expressing as never before how ideas flow and interrelate, how the subconscious is made manifest. Wagner, as we know, was acutely aware of the fructifying power of myth, but also of myth's ability to portray deep psychological trauma, which he could now portray with great subtlety: a nexus of motifs in sound could now convey that which perhaps had been imperfectly grasped in the mind.[7]

Power – and lust. The young Richard Wagner saw in sexuality the highest manifestation of love between a man and a woman and deplored the stultifying strictures of marriage and proprietorial transactions. The subjugation of woman he found repulsive: Alberich's gloating threat that the pretty women who had spurned his wooing would succumb to him as owner of the ring, Sieglinde's lament that she had been reduced to a mere chattel in *Die Walküre* and, later, the deception played upon Brünnhilde to trick her into Gunther's bed are anathema. Consanguinity? Fricka, the wife of Wotan and goddess of marriage, is appalled, but the love music Wagner would compose for *Die Walküre* is some of the most moving in the whole cycle. It is love which irradiates this drama, of man for woman, of god for peccant daughter; in *Das Rheingold* there is none. That work amazes by its swimming maidens, its aquamarine light and golden gleam, its giants, gods and sulphurous Nibelheim, eighteen manic anvils, shattering hammer-blow and sparkling rainbow bridge; it is also a portrayal of a loveless world, full of deceit, threat, vindictiveness, greed, curses and violence. It has a discredited god, ostensible guarantor of treaties, who is sullenly forced to relinquish the ring he has stolen by guile in order to save Freia, goddess of youth, without whom the gods would dwindle and fade. The gods' subsequent procession across the rainbow bridge to Valhalla has an empty bluster about it, a hollow, self-deluding triumphalism. Wotan brushes aside the Rheinmaidens' lament from below, for he has conceived a plan – and the glittering sword motif arises from the orchestra as from the depths of his mind. He will beget a hero who, not bound by treaties, will restore the ring to him.

We must wait until *Die Walküre* to meet human beings in the ecstasy of love and the tragedy of loss, when a Valkyrie becomes a woman and sees what true love entails. Here the glories of *music* drama are experienced to an unparalleled degree, surpassing even *Lohengrin* in the sheer power and beauty of sound, the most intense expression of emotion. The first act of *Die Walküre* is one of the most moving in the whole of the *Ring* as Siegmund and Sieglinde, twins begotten by Wotan on a mortal woman, and separated as children, now joyfully come together and consecrate their incestuous love as Hunding, Sieglinde's husband, lies drugged upstairs. In Bryan Magee's words: 'Not only utterly abandoned love, but the discon-certingly emotional nakedness and vulnerability that go with it are uninhibitedly expressed . . . what reaches us here in the audience is something that has never before found expression in art.'[8] In the orgiastic climax Siegfried will be conceived, but the joy of the twins will be short-lived. In Act Two Wotan's immense soliloquy leads to our seeing him in a new and more sympathetic light, disturbing in his acknowledgement that he now sought nothing but the end, oblivion. One of Wagner's most heart-wrenching moments is Wotan's farewell, at the end of Act Three, to his beloved child as he kisses her godhead from her and protects her sleeping form in a ring of magic fire. He has also, we must not forget, been forced to submit to his wife's imperious demand that he order the death of his son.

Das Ende: eternal rest, oblivion. What is happening here? The famous letter to Röckel (25–26 January 1854)extolling the joys of sexual love also explains the following:

An illustration (after a drawing by Knut Ekwall) of the second act of *Die Walküre* (1854–6).

We must learn *to die and to die* in the fullest sense of the word . . . Wodan (sic) rises to the tragic height of *willing* his own destruction. This is all that we need to know from the history of mankind: *to will what is necessary* and to bring it about ourselves.

It should be born in mind that these dark thoughts *predate* Wagner's reading of Schopenhauer, whose masterpiece *Die Welt als Wille und Vorstellung* (*The World as Will and Idea*) Wagner would read, on Herwegh's recommendation, in the autumn of 1854. Wagner would later claim that during a reading of this work, he was 'amazed' to find that his Nibelung poem somehow confirmed, even anticipated, what Schopenhauer was saying; only then did he truly understand his own Wotan and, greatly shaken, he went on to a closer study of Schopenhauer's philosophy.[9] Schopenhauer will be of greater interest to us during a discussion of *Tristan und Isolde,* the first conception of which dates from that remarkable year, 1854, during whose October he was composing the music for Act Three of *Die Walküre.* A letter to Liszt of 16(?) December 1854 again refers to Schopenhauer in glowing terms as 'the greatest philosopher since Kant . . . His principal idea, the final denial of the will to live, is of terrible seriousness, but it is uniquely redeeming' (it also airily explains that 'it did not strike me as anything new').[10]

The turmoil of Wagner's growing passion for Mathilde Wesendonck, and the plans for a work on *Tristan und Isolde* ('the simplest but most full-blooded musical composition') preoccupied him more and more; the completion of *Die Walküre* was put on hold, but before Wagner could turn to the composition of *Tristan und Isolde*, a work which, he hoped, would be easy to stage and perhaps even earn him some money, an invitation from the Old Philharmonic Society to come to London and conduct a series of concerts was, perhaps ill-advisedly, accepted.

John William Waterhouse, *Tristram and Isolde Sharing the Potion*, c. 1916, oil on canvas.

The reasons for going were naturally financial; Wagner stayed for five months and bitterly regretted it (he lived, he claimed, like a damned soul in Hell). Things went badly from the start: Wagner soon learned that the English musical scene was run on commercial, not aesthetic, lines and this was entirely antithetical to his idealism.

Rehearsals were far too short, and the programmes were frequently not to his liking: often a hotch-potch of overtures, concertos and symphonies which he felt to be beneath him. The tradition of wearing kid gloves he also found irksome, and here is the place to dispel once and for all the unpleasant canard that he, an anti-Semite, could only conduct Mendelssohn wearing kid gloves for fear of contamination before removing them to conduct his beloved Weber. His third concert in Hanover Square on 16 April 1855 consisted of Mendelssohn's 'Italian' Symphony, an aria from Spohr's *Faust*, Beethoven's Second Piano Concerto, a Mozart aria and the overture to Weber's *Euryanthe*. Wagner was often cavalier about wearing the gloves, sometimes wearing them when entering the hall but then removing them before playing. At this particular concert he amused his German friends sitting in the audience (Ferdinand Praeger and Karl Lüders) by keeping the gloves on for Mendelssohn but also for Spohr, Beethoven and Mozart, then finally removing them for *Euryanthe*. He was thus showing his indifference to the Philharmonic's tradition: it was up to *him* whether or not he wore gloves, and Mendelssohn's Jewishness had nothing to do with it. His indifference to the social proprieties also meant that he refused to make the rounds of the influential music critics in return for their kind recommendation or 'puffs', and consequently received bad reviews.

He gave eight concerts in all; Queen Victoria and Prince Albert came to the seventh. Wagner, Rupert Christiansen explains, was 'susceptible to such gracious royal attention, as radical socialists tend to be'.[11] Wagner wrote a lively letter to his wife about his meeting with the royal couple, their obvious approval of the *Tannhäuser* overture and Prince Albert's inability to agree with the queen's suggestion that his operas be translated into Italian: Albert opined that Italian singers would have no idea how to sing them.[12] But these pleasantries were the notable exception to the rule: the redoubtable James Davison, music critic of *The*

'Tristan und Isolde', a postcard reproduction after a painting by Franz Stassen.

Times, was ruthless in his condemnation of Wagner's work. Instead of earning a princely sum, Wagner came away with only 10,000 francs (some £40) profit. This was, he would insist, the hardest money he had ever earned; he had had to pay for every one of these francs with a feeling of bitterness which, he hoped, it would never fall to him to experience again. But he had somehow continued to work at the orchestration of *Die Walküre* and, later that year, conceived of *Tristan und Isolde* as a three-act drama in which the dying Tristan would be visited by the wanderer Parzival; this Tristan, wishing to die yet unable to, becomes identified with Amfortas in the story of the Grail.[13]

Unique, surely, in the history of music is the fecundity of Wagner's mind, the jostling plans and possibilities: Tristan, and indeed Parsifal, approach the world of Siegfried. Then, in May 1856, Wagner wrote down a prose sketch of a Buddhist drama to be entitled *Die Sieger* (The Victors), a work which extols renunciation. This idea derives from Schopenhauer and Eugène Burnouf's *Introduction à l'histoire du buddhisme indien*, in which Wagner found a story which made a deep impression on him. Savitri, a lowly Chandala girl, meets Buddha's favourite disciple Ananda and falls passionately in love with him. She approaches Buddha and begs to be allowed to unite with Ananda. Buddha consents on condition that she joins in his disciples' vow of chastity. The Buddha knows of Savitri's earlier incarnation: she had been a wealthy Brahmin's daughter who had arrogantly rejected the love of a prince. Her punishment was to be reborn into a lower caste and she must now suffer the pains of unrequited love. Only through renunciation can she be redeemed and received into the community of Buddha. The girl joyfully accepts this condition and is welcomed by Ananda as a sister. The draft ends with the words: 'Buddha's last teachings. All profess his religion. He wanders towards the place of his deliverance (*Erlösung*).'[14] It is strange that the world of *Parsifal* should be adumbrated here;

three different worlds (*Parsifal*, *Tristan und Isolde* and *Siegfried*), then, but unmistakeably interlocked. Young, fatherless heroes are in all three and, shared among two others, are heroines with healing powers, young hunters, a kiss which radically changes the recipient, a woman insulted to be used against her will and an act of self-immolation over a dead man.[15]

How tempting it must have been for Wagner, with his passionate desire for another man's wife (Savitri and Ananda seem very remote), to let rip a portrayal of illicit love in music of terrifying intensity. But he disciplined himself and turned his attention to the *Ring* once more, completing the first orchestral sketch of Act One of *Siegfried*; a blacksmith living opposite him on the Zeltweg infuriated him with his hammering but also provided him with a motif for Siefried's sword-forging and furious outburst against the dwarf Mime. On 22 October Liszt's 53rd birthday was celebrated in the familiar Hotel Baur au Lac with an improvised 'performance' of Act One of *Die Walküre* with Wagner as Siegmund and Hunding, a certain Frau Emilie Heim as Sieglinde and Liszt at the piano.

At the end of the year *Siegfried* received Wagner's full attention and he was much preoccupied by the orchestral sketches for Acts One and Two. On 19 December, however, the first musical themes to *Tristan und Isolde* were also jotted down, including a chromatically rising theme of yearning; four months later the Wagners moved to a small summer house named the 'Asyl', or refuge, in the grounds of the as yet unfinished Wesendonck villa on the so-called 'Green Hill' near Zurich.

Siegfried is that part of the *Ring* most indebted to German Romanticism, with its forest, dwarf, dragon, magic helmet, ring and woodbird; the young hero who sets forth to learn the meaning of fear steps from the pages of the Brothers Grimm. We meet again Mime, Alberich's wretched kinsman, deep in the forests where he had brought up the young Siegfried, born to the dying Sieglinde. It is fashionable now to portray Siegfried as an adolescent bully;

Knut Ekwall, 'Brunnhilde's Awakening', 1876, from Act Three of *Siegfried* (1856–7).

'Siegfried on his Bier', 1876, from Act Three of *Götterdammerung* (1869–74), the final opera in the Ring cycle.

there is much youthful exuberance in him, but also much tenderness when he thinks of the mother he never knew, thinking that her eyes may have been that of a doe; he also thinks of his father, for he knows that Mime can never be this. Mime is hardly a model of loving kindness despite his plangent insistence that he, a poor old dwarf, brought up a whimpering babe who is now a man; his plan is to bring Siegfried up so that he may kill the dragon Fafner who guards the hoard containing the Tarnhelm and the ring. He tries desperately to forge the remnants of Siegmund's sword with which the dying Sieglinde had entrusted him, but fails. At the end of Act One the young Siegfried, disgusted with the dwarf, forges the sword anew and shatters the anvil before rushing into the forest to slay the dragon. He accomplishes this in Act Two and kills the dragon and Mime, who has brewed a poison to kill him. Seizing both ring and Tarnhelm, he listens to the woodbird who tells him of a wondrous woman asleep on a fire-girt mountain. And the woodbird guides him there.

Twelve years would elapse between the completion of this Act and the writing of Act Three, that overwhelming Act in which the young hero confronts his grandfather Wotan and shatters his spear before awakening the sleeping Brünnhilde. In an ecstasy of joy, the two consummate their love. The music would become richer, denser here, the leitmotifs contrapuntally interwoven into unforgettable patterns of sound. Wagner would, between Acts Two and Three, write two gigantic masterpieces, *Tristan und Isolde* and *Die Meistersinger von Nürnberg*, yet could also successfully work his way back, as it were, into the fabric of the *Ring*. Already in Acts One and Two of *Siegfried* the listener becomes aware of the prominence of the orchestra. Now, in Act Three, a huge edifice of sound has been created, blending the leitmotifs of the earlier acts and moderating them with great subtlety.[16] And the orchestra, it seems, supplants the vocal line in its immense ability to convey the inner significance of what is happening on stage, with thousands of repetitions of motifs weaving and interlocking. Will the love of Siegfried and Brünnhilde triumph over a corrupt world? Will the gold finally return to the Rhine? We do not as yet know, but we do know that the music transcends all else, and for that it is Schopenhauer that we must thank.

Wagner devoured Schopenhauer's masterpiece *Die Welt als Wille und Vorstellung* five times in just over one and a half years; he referred to Schopenhauer innumerable times throughout his life and Cosima's diaries are shot through with Wagner's comments on him. The consequences of this study of Schopenhauer were far-reaching, even convulsive, for Wagner's works would from now on move in a markedly different direction. His eyes were opened to what he had truly known all along, despite his earlier intellectual insistence on what he would know as the 'Greek' view of the world, a view sustained by Feuerbach and the politics of Röckel and Bakunin. *My Life* tells us that there was no sustenance whatever in Schopenhauer for those seeking in philosophy a justification for left-wing political agitation: Schopenhauer saw more deeply into the very nature of the world.[17] For Schopenhauer, absolute reality, the Kantian *Ding an sich* (thing in itself), was what he called the Will, a blind, furious and relentless striving for existence which may be transcended either by utter self-abnegation (the way of the saint) or by the transfiguration of the Will into an *idea*: that is, an object of aesthetic contemplation. To stand outside the meaningless thrust of existence, to recreate it objectively, is the privilege of the artist in his inspired moments, and it is the *musician* above all who claims our attention here. For whereas the representational arts simply imitate the various manifestations of the Will in phenomena, music, which does not rely on images and concepts, represents more directly the Will itself, not its exterior manifestations. And Schopenhauer now, by a remarkable sleight of hand, proclaims that music is both the art form closest to the Will and its miraculous transformation into form and harmony: a reflection of senselessness, it miraculously *transfigures* senselessness. A logical flaw, perhaps, but many a structure of considerable aesthetic merit would be built upon it in the nineteenth century.[18]

Schopenhauer came as a revelation to Wagner. But Wagner was now faced by almost insurmountable difficulties. The poem of the *Ring*, comprising *Das Rheingold*, *Die Walküre*, *Siegfried* and *Götterdämmerung*, had been published, albeit privately, and he had embarked upon the creation of a music drama of gigantic size in which many of his earlier social and political ideas were to become manifest. What Wagner – already before reading Schopenhauer – had seen, however, in his Wotan was a figure longing for extinction; now Schopenhauer was telling him of the fatality of all striving and that Nirvana, self-abnegation, was the supreme goal. He toyed with this theme in the draft for *Die Sieger*, but the *Ring* poem stood there for all the world to see, and it derived unambiguously from his days as a political radical: Siegfried and Brünnhilde, representing free love, would triumph over a debased world. Wagner had also insisted in his numerous essays and in a major book that music had no special status but would be an equal partner with the arts and had written one drama, *Das Rheingold*, to exemplify this. He had, then, committed himself both privately and publicly to principles that were at odds with Schopenhauer's philosophy.[19] This realization may well have broken a lesser man: Wagner, however, stood firm, insisting that his portrayal of Wotan predated the reading of Schopenhauer. In later life, on 29 March 1878, he even boasted to Cosima that Schopenhauer would have been amazed that Wagner had been able to portray Wotan without reading him.[20] This is yet another example of Wagner's tenacity and truculence; he balked at the onerous task of unstitching the fabric of the published *Ring* but would later, as we shall see in *Götterdämmerung*, graft different endings on to it, some more satisfactory than others.

But in 1859, the struggle with the colossal *Ring* material, its cumbersome shape and seemingly intractable difficulties, was put aside; Wagner explained to Liszt that he had left *Siegfried* beneath a linden tree and that his energies were now directed at composing a short work, easily performable, which would be a success in the opera house: it was to be on *Tristan und Isolde*. First a few biographical details: the relationship between Wagner and Mathilde was growing in intensity; in September 1857 Hans von Bülow passed through Zurich on his honeymoon and three women sat at Wagner's table: Mathilde, Minna and Bülow's bride Cosima. Wagner played passages from *Siegfried* on the piano at which Cosima wept. Some two weeks later Wagner finished the first draft of the *Tristan* poem and handed it to Mathilde, who identified the passion of the lovers with the passion which she knew was developing between Wagner and herself. Hans and Cosima von Bülow travelled to Berlin with a copy of the complete *Tristan* poem and, on 1 October, Wagner started to write down the music for Act One. He thereby took music into realms almost unthinkable, passing into harmonic complexities which would precipitate a crisis in tonality and characterize much of twentieth-century music. Or, to quote a diary entry of Richard Strauss, the work 'absorbed the whole of Romanticism, leading to its supreme culmination', at the same time 'placing a divine copestone upon it with the most beautifully orchestrated B major chord in the whole history of music'.[21]

Wagner knew his medieval sources; he was also able to conceive the idea for the work in 1854, a few weeks after reading Schopenhauer. Attention has been drawn to the possible influence of Hans von Bülow's orchestral fantasy *Nirwana*, with its prefigurement of the rising chromatic phrasing to be found in *Tristan*.[22] Wagner certainly knew Bülow's work, which was originally conceived as an overture to a tragedy of the same name by Karl Ritter (Ritter, son of Wagner's Dresden benefactress Julie Ritter, was an overwrought young man who had accompanied Wagner into exile in Switzerland and visits to Venice: he had once concluded an abortive suicide pact with Cosima von Bülow, and the subject-matter of *Nirwana* was also flippantly known as the 'Suicide Fantasia'). Ritter's flawed attempt to dramatize the Tristan legend may well have been recalled by Wagner in his 1854 sketch, as well as Bülow's own music, but with the 'Tristan chord' Wagner entered an utterly different world.

The 'Tristan chord', that haunting half-dominant seventh chord made up of a minor third, a diminished fifth and a minor seventh, has entered musical history as the epitome of longing, longing which is only resolved at the end of the work after three searing acts which push Tristan's longing for Isolde and for death to an unprecedented intensity. (Whether this chord is presaged in earlier composers such as Mozart, Spohr, Liszt or Berlioz is unimportant: it is the intensity of Wagner's music, its almost unparalleled expression of sexual longing and ultimate resolution, which is very much his own.) That which was meant to be an unassuming work, a potboiler even, would enter the repertoire as one of the most intense, difficult and erotic works in musical history, an intensely gripping psychological and emotional drama. And Wagner would become increasingly aware of the work's problematic nature; writing to Mathilde Wesendonck from Venice in April 1859, he suggests, half jokingly, that the opera's last act is so terrifying that it might be banned for fear of driving people insane. A work based on medieval legend but now, in the second half of the nineteenth century, would shock and overwhelm as never before. Yet this most 'sexual' of dramas is shot through with death and ultimate transfiguration; it is unthinkable without the work of Arthur Schopenhauer.[23] Never before in music drama had such an erotic charge been sustained by such a death rapture, a sympathy with death suffused from first to last by a philosophical system.

For Schopenhauer the path to redemption, release from this world, lies in renunciation, self-abnegation and the transformation of brute sexuality into *caritas*, or pity. But Wagner, in his passion for Mathilde, could not accept his philosophical idol's belief. In an earlier letter to Mathilde he speaks of a need to correct 'my friend Schopenhauer', particularly the latter's metaphysics of sexual love. Schopenhauer argued that death is to be welcomed as a liberation from selfish self-preservation and from a sexuality linked to the Will's ultimate goal: that is, procreation. But for Wagner sexual love is no longer tied to any such goal but is identified with the longing for death, a state in which individual barriers are transcended and the individual merges into a union with the totality of all. In ecstatic union, Tristan and Isolde are one; together in death they find ultimate fulfilment. In Wagner's extraordinary music drama, it is not through self-abnegation but through sexual rapture that Schopenhauer's brute Will is transcended; there is no mere obliteration but a union, rapt and mystical, a merging into a pantheistic vision. Nietzsche, in one of his posthumously published fragments, saw this quite clearly: 'In *Tristan* love should be interpreted not as Schopenhauerian but Empedoclean', he explained, 'for such love was the sign and guarantee of an eternal unity'.[24]

Leaving metaphysics to one side, *Tristan und Isolde* is acknowledged by many to be the ultimate among Wagner's works, the summit and supreme crisis of Romantic music, more thoroughly *musical* in its tonal brilliance than any he had hitherto attempted. Schopenhauer had convinced Wagner of the supremacy of music: Act Two is almost one long symphonic poem and vocal duet. There is almost no action and the words are 'little more than sonant carriers for the musical tones, without conceptual significance'.[25] The music, chromatically and harmonically more daring than anything Wagner had written before, triumphs over all. Leitmotifs tend now to become elusive in their associations, almost non-specific; the self-absorption of both Tristan and Isolde, the unresolved dissonances, suspensions, raving deliriums, take the listener into intensities unequalled before or since.[26] Everywhere is the sea, the infinite, and the final transfiguration of the lovers, together with the ultimate resolution of that troubling 'Tristan chord', takes us into an ascension, an experience almost religious, a redemption not brought about by God but by human love of a unique and unforgettable kind, a mystical union within a pantheistically spiritualized universe.

In Zurich, meanwhile, Wagner's involvement with Mathilde was causing much marital discord: at the end of 1857 Wagner had presented her with the compositional sketch of *Tristan und Isolde* with a dedication to the Angel who had 'elevated him to the height'. He also (and this was very unusual – he had not written any songs since setting Heine and others during his earlier Parisian days) composed a series of songs based on her poems: these would later be known as the *Wesendonck Lieder* and were unmistakenly drenched in the heady atmosphere of *Tristan*. On 7 April of the following year, 1858, he sent a letter to Mathilde containing a pencil sketch of the prelude to *Tristan und Isolde* which ended with the exhortation that she should 'take all of his soul as a greeting to the morning!' This was intercepted and read by Minna, who demanded an explanation; in vain Wagner sought to convince her of the platonic nature of the relationship. She informed the Wesendoncks of her suspicions. The days in the 'Asyl' were numbered and Wagner, together with Karl Ritter, travelled to Venice to escape the sultry atmosphere and recriminations at home.

Wagner became the sole occupant of the Palazzo Giustiniani. The lugubrious call of the gondoliers, the sombre brackish canals and the black gondolas, the alternating desire for oblivion and the intense yearning for Mathilde (were they not two pilgrims on the way to extinction?), together with the constant threats from police surveillance (for Venice was now under Austrian rule and the Austrians had been informed of the arrival of this erstwhile renegade), the feelings of isolation, of having pushed his art to the very limits of what had hitherto been acceptable – all united to form a unique pattern, and much of the music of *Tristan* was composed here. In Wagner's absence, before vacating the Asyl house, finding it impossible to remain there, his wife wrote to Mathilde that she felt the need, with bleeding heart, to remind Frau Wesendonck that she had succeeded in separating her husband from her after almost 22 years of marriage. May that noble deed, she finished, contribute to your peace of mind and to your satisfaction.[27] Wagner meanwhile, in a diary kept for Mathilde, spoke rapturously about *Tristan*, of the incomparable intensity of the music and of his desire to see her again and comfort her. If they were no longer Tristan and Isolde they must become Savitri and Ananda, living in Buddhistic renunciation: this Wagner implies in a series of letters he wrote to her from Venice between August and December 1858. Insufferable posing perhaps, but also of interest, in that the Buddhistic elements will prepare the way for *Parsifal*. He has also, he claims, dissolved Venice into music, the music of a dream; the Austrian authorities, however, demanded his extradition. The Governor of Lombardy, Archduke Maximilian, granted an extension to Wagner's permit, and Wagner finally left the city in March 1859.

The years between 1859 and 1864 are best described as Wagner's *Wanderjahre*, years of restless uncertainty and often desperate attempts to solve his financial and emotional difficulties. On 1 August 1859, at half past four in the afternoon, he finished the score of *Tristan und Isolde* (the same day, incidentally, that Dresden experienced its premiere of *Lohengrin*). The relationship between him and the Wesendoncks had been restored or at least regulated, and Wagner spent three days in the Wesendonck residence, meeting Herwegh, the writer Gottfried Keller and Semper again. In the same month he returned again to Paris, the city which still dazzled him, even though he hated it, where he hoped desperately to stage

Tannhäuser. He moved into a house at 16, rue Newton, and hired domestic servants as well as a valet. Here he sought to save his marriage and invited Minna to join him, promising, on her demand, to abstain from sexual intercourse; she arrived with dog and parrot, dismissed the servants and scolded him for his luxurious lifestyle.

In January 1860 the first of his three Wagner concerts took place with the Entry of the Nobles from Act Two of *Tannhäuser*, excerpts from *Lohengrin*, the overture to *Der fliegende Holländer* and the prelude to *Tristan und Isolde*; those present included Auber, Berlioz, Gounod – and Meyerbeer. The next two concerts were a resounding success, and Wagner's salon welcomed Saint-Saëns, Gounod, Baroness Malwida von Meysenbug (a German writer and political activist), Gustave Doré, Catulle Mendès (the future husband of Judith Gautier) and many others who would later form the nucleus of the *Revue fantaisiste* with its ardent championship of Wagner. More importantly, they would also prepare the way for the idolatry of the *Revue wagnérienne*.[28] After the concerts, on 17 February, Baudelaire wrote an enthusiastic letter to Wagner explaining that he owed the composer the greatest musical joy that he had ever experienced, and that it had seemed to Baudelaire that *he* had written this music. The poet of *Les Fleurs du mal* sensed that here, in Wagner, was an artist capable of overwhelming, indeed, overpowering his audience: the poem 'La musique' seemed to describe perfectly this forceful ravishing.[29] It would also be Baudelaire who, a year later, would leap to Wagner's defence after the scandalous uproar surrounding the performance of *Tannhäuser* which *did* take place at the Opéra.

It was Napoleon III who commissioned the work. The princess Pauline Metternich, Wagner enthusiast and wife of the Austrian ambassador, brought her influence to bear on the Empress Eugénie, who requested that the Emperor demand a performance. This decree, however, would fall foul of the anti-German element in the aristocracy, who would do their utmost to wreck the piece. Wagner set to work to compose a fresh bacchanal, the Dresden version seeming too pallid to him now. A letter to Mathilde explains that the French are talented but incredibly decadent; the race must be developed and ennobled, and his *Tannhäuser* will be a matter of the most vital concern for the educability of these people.[30] The French, he continues, are not a musical race; poetry also was completely alien to a race that only knew rhetoric and eloquence. The French must be taught what music can do and he, Wagner, is going to show them by composing a great ballet in which he will portray the horrors of the Venusberg. People, he concludes, are going to be amazed at what he has hatched up here . . .

After 164 rehearsals *Tannhäuser* was staged on 13 March 1861; the riot of that opening night has passed into musical history. The Jockey Club, a group of aristocrats inimical to the Court, used the excuse of having to watch a ballet in Act One – instead of dining, as was usual, with the prettiest girls of the corps de ballet and having the ballet in Act Two – to demonstrate against this German composer with whistles and flageolets. Dietsch, the conductor, was in Bülow's opinion a mean stupid ass, a geriatric with no memory and no intelligence who was completely beyond help. The second night was worse than the first; the ballet had been totally misunderstood by the maître de ballet Lucien Petipa (brother of the more famous Marius) who had only used the second rank of dancers, not the principals. Wagner refused to attend the third performance, which had to be stopped for a quarter of an hour, then immediately withdrew the work in disgust. (Vindictively, some ten years later, during the Franco-Prussian war, Wagner wanted Paris bombarded and burnt to the ground, while Cosima delighted in the thought that for every bar of *Tannhäuser* the Parisians booed they were now, in 1870 getting a condign Prussian reply in the form of cannonade.)

Returning to Germany, Wagner visited Karlsruhe, where he met the Grand Duke and Duchess in a private audience; the possibility of a *Tannhäuser* performance there was mooted. Or Vienna? Wagner travelled there next to put out feelers; the Vienna opera could not agree but held out the possibility of a future premiere. And Wagner had the joyful experience of seeing his *Lohengrin* performed there to thunderous acclamation.

Meanwhile Otto Wesendonck's magnanimity and tacit acceptance of his wife's special if incomprehensible relationship with the composer was evident in his invitation to Wagner to accompany the couple to Trieste and thence by ship to Venice; here Wagner stood in rapture before Titian's *Assumption of the Virgin* in the Accademia.[31] He wrote in *My Life* that his old creative powers had reawakened before such a masterpiece: 'I decided to compose *Die Meistersinger*.'[32] On the train journey back to Vienna, he conceived with great clarity the best part of the C major overture and worked on the drama throughout the rest of the year.

In February 1862 he gave one of his now favourite readings to a group gathered at the publisher Franz Schott's residence, the composer Peter Cornelius having made the irksome journey from Mainz for the sole purpose of hearing it. (The pedantic town clerk is here given the name of Hans Lich, a pointed reference to the music critic Eduard Hanslick, who was also present and who was not known as a defender of the Wagner cause.) Wagner was now in a buoyant mood, but a visit from Minna and a barrage of recriminations ended what he could only describe to Cornelius as ten days of hell. But work on *Die Meistersinger* continued: on his birthday, 22 May, Wagner conceived the prelude to Act Three and brought it to paper. It is amazing indeed that after composing *Tristan und Isolde*, which took nineteenth-century music to realms scarcely dreamt of, he should absorb the structures of J. S. Bach and recreate the world of the Reformation with a chorale and the use of triple counterpoint and double fugue. This will be considered in the next chapter; suffice it to say here that some of the most accessible of all Wagner's music was germinating despite the

growing awareness that *Tristan* had assumed an immensely problematic stature and that the cumbersome *Ring* material was likely to
be consigned to oblivion. His debts were becoming unmanageable;
his marriage, a tragedy. But female company was not something he
could live without. Many women were attracted to him, to his
energy, genius and ebullience, and many proved difficult to resist.

He was drawn to Mathilde Maier, a lawyer's daughter who
seemed to play the role of Eva to his Hans Sachs: he tried to persuade
her to live with him as housekeeper and consoling angel, but her
incipient deafness made her reluctant to become too deeply involved.
There was an intimate flirtation with Blandine Ollivier, wife of the
French politician, and with Seraphine Mauro, niece of his friend
Dr Joseph Standhartner, much to the annoyance of Peter Cornelius,
her lover. A letter to Mathilde Wesendonck spoke of the need for
a daughter, and during his Vienna sojourn he took in a charming
seventeen-year-old girl to serve him his tea and to be present at the
table in the evening, but this girl did not relish the company of a
fifty-year-old voluptuary and fled. It was her older sister, Maria
Völkl, who took over the role of housekeeper and perhaps more;
she was urged in a letter from Breslau to have his room suitably
warmed and perfumed, and this is the letter which refers, tantalizingly, to the 'pink drawers' which Wagner hoped would be ready.[33]
Far more serious, of course, would be a growing – and reciprocal
– affection for the wife of Hans von Bülow: Cosima found herself
trapped in a loveless marriage, and Wagner's magnetic presence
she would find increasingly fascinating and disturbing. Mathilde
Wesendonck may well have written to Wagner that the weft of the
mysterious weaver who intertwined the threads of their mysterious
fate was never to be unravelled, but only to be torn asunder, but
it was obvious that Wagner was drawing away from such esoteric
fantasies, fantasies which he himself had encouraged.

At the end of 1862 he published a preface to the edition of *Der
Ring des Nibelungen* that would appear the following year, stressing

again the need for a festival in a small town, the building of an amphitheatre and an invisible orchestra which would be financed – somehow. By a prince, perhaps? Would this prince be forthcoming? In the spring of 1863 he travelled to St Petersburg to give a series of concerts at a Philharmonic Society; there was also a benefit concert at the Imperial Opera House. There were three concerts in Moscow; he returned, exhausted, with 7,000 thaler. After paying off his most pressing debts, support for his wife and the furbishment of a luxurious apartment with silks, satins, pillows, lace and sundry extravagances, he was left with very little of it. He nevertheless finished the score of the first scene of *Die Meistersinger* and conducted concerts in Budapest; in November he visited the Wesendoncks for the last time but was not pleased to learn that there could be no further talk of financial support. On 28 November he arrived in Berlin and in the afternoon, went for a drive with Cosima. *My Life* describes how they gazed mutely into each other's eyes, and then an intense longing for the fullest avowal of their love forced them to a confession: 'With tears and sobs we sealed a vow to ourselves alone.'[34]

It is obvious that his life was approaching a crisis. To flee his more aggressive creditors he left for Zurich; passing through Munich on Good Friday he stood before a shop window which showed a portrayal of the young Bavarian king who, at eighteen years old, had succeeded Maximilian II four weeks earlier. He lodged with Eliza Wille and her husband; he confided to Peter Cornelius that only a miracle could save him now. Dr Wille demonstrated an undeniable coolness towards him; a letter to Mathilde Wesendonck had also been returned unopened. He was now at the end of his tether and left for Stuttgart hoping that the conductor there, Karl Eckert, being well disposed towards him, might help to find a quiet spot where he could complete the orchestration of the first act of *Die Meistersinger*. Eckert was certainly cordial, but Wagner was unsettled by a card left for

Richard Wagner in 1864.

him by the secretary of the king of Bavaria. He ignored it, sensing something disagreeable, and returned to his hotel where he learned that a gentleman wished to meet him on a very urgent matter. A meeting was arranged for the following morning at ten o'clock.

In his darkest moment he had come to the bitter conclusion that only a miracle – a wealthy patron or prince, say – could save him. The miracle had indeed happened: one who had now ascended to the throne was waiting.

5

World Fame

Wagner's work is a veritable eruption of talent and genius, the profoundly serious yet enchanting work of a sensuous sorcerer, drunk with his own wisdom.

Thomas Mann

'*Ein Wunder! Ein Wunder ist gekommen! Ein unerhörtes, nie gesehenes Wunder!*' 'A miracle has happened! Unheard of, never seen before!' These words from *Lohengrin* seem apt to describe Wagner's emotions as he stood before the young king of Bavaria in the early afternoon of 4 May in the Munich *Residenz*. The young man idolized him, giving him wealth, peace of mind and the opportunity to complete his life's work; he had been lifted from penury and lack of recognition and was now triumphant. Had ever such amazing good fortune befallen a musician before? He was given a ring, a signed photograph of the King and the assurance of royal patronage and love; such a moment, such a peripeteia has been endlessly told, endlessly portrayed as a fairy tale, an event surrounded by a romantic nimbus worthy of operettas. However, the whole episode of Wagner's relationship with Ludwig II became increasingly fraught, tawdry and occasionally downright duplicitous: Wagner could even refer to his royal saviour as a cretin (to Cosima, on 5 November 1869) and Ludwig, lost, bewildered and touchingly munificent, would move increasingly into a world of shadows and fantasies.

King Ludwig II of Bavaria.

As a fifteen-year-old Ludwig had seen *Lohengrin* at the Court Theatre in Munich and this changed his life forever. His interest in Wagner's work was not musical, but the world which Wagner had created, of swan and dove, of radiant knight and sacerdotal mysteries, its poeticizing of history and transformation of reality into myth – all this fascinated him. With Wagner now at his side he could forget the tedious world of court etiquette, of politics, of quotidian reality, and escape into a world of wondrous beauty, a realm which would be exemplified in the building of Neuschwanstein, Hunding's hut, the Venusberg and the mechanical swan which could draw him across silver waters.

Wagner was naturally dazzled by the amazing good fortune which had brought him a king's devotion and acted the part of devout and awed recipient of royal beneficence and ecstatic effusions. The King addressed him as 'My most fervent beloved!' 'My most beloved, glorious friend!' Wagner would reply. This overwrought, reverential tone became more extreme: the King addressed Wagner as 'My all! Epitome of felicity!'; 'Sublime, divine friend!'; 'Saviour who enraptures me!'; 'Primal source of the light of life!' Wagner's replies were similarly euphoric, but one senses that for him it was simply play-acting, living up to what was expected of him. Later, on 10 July 1873, Cosima drew his attention to the artificial tone he was using when writing to the King, and Wagner admitted that the tone was indeed inauthentic but insisted that he was not the instigator. The enraptured outpourings of undying affection were all very well, but stresses and strains became increasingly evident. Wagner may, initially, have felt happy to join in the charade, but whereas Ludwig was utterly transported, Wagner was forced to play his part with circumspection, for he needed the King's adoration – and his resources – more and more.

The happiest time for Ludwig was when Wagner was billeted close to him in Haus Pellet on the Starnberger See; he was fascinated by Wagner's plans and vowed to help in any possible way. It was here that Cosima von Bülow visited Wagner and their union was sealed. In September Wagner moved into a handsome house in Munich's Brienner Strasse in which he could indulge his lavish needs for opulent furnishings (there was much white, rose and grey satin, lace, yellow silk and softly upholstered couches perfumed with attar of roses). He also worked at the orchestration of *Siegfried*'s second act; the King showed his delight by promising Wagner a festival theatre of vast proportions for the *Ring* cycle and the composer, initially overwhelmed, suggested his erstwhile colleague Semper as the architect. But rumours were spreading throughout the city about his sybaritic lifestyle, the substantial sums he was costing the Bavarian treasury and what was said to be his baleful influence over the King: just as Ludwig's grandfather, Ludwig I, had succumbed to the charms of the Irish adventuress Lola Montez (Eliza Gilbert), so now his grandson was under the spell of a Saxon renegade nicknamed 'Lolus'. The prime minister, Karl Ludwig Freiherr von der Pfordten, abhorred Wagner and attacked his arrogance and profligacy. Further rumours were also circulating concerning Wagner's relations with Hans von Bülow's wife, who gave birth on 10 April to Wagner's first child, a daughter to be named Isolde; it was on that day that her cuckolded husband began the first orchestral rehearsals of *Tristan und Isolde*. And this work, after considerable difficulties, received its premiere in the presence of the King on 10 June 1865, with Ludwig Schnorr von Carolsfeld and his wife Malwine in the leading roles. It was, artistically, a triumph but the critics spoke of disharmony and shamelessness; the libretto was an absurdity and the music was the sophisticated concoction of a decayed, sick imagination. In July, however, Wagner was stunned to hear of the death of Schnorr, whose distracted widow held Wagner responsible.[1] After a temporary cooling of his relationship with the King (Wagner is reported to have referred to him, in the presence of others, as '*Mein Junge*' [young man]), Wagner was again received by Ludwig, who longed to hear of any progress in the writing of *Parzival* (the original spelling). He prevaricated and started to draft a series of essays entitled '*Was ist deutsch?*' (What is German?), which claim that the German spirit is best understood as being present where beauty and nobility, esteemed for themselves and not for the sake of any advantage, may be found (x, p. 97); attacks are also made on foreign (Jewish and French) influences and alien notions of democracy. The King bestowed 44,000 florins on Wagner; the treasury, incensed, condescended to pay in coin, which Cosima had to transport in a carriage through the streets and which naturally caused much interest and annoyance among the populace.

In November Wagner was Ludwig's guest in Hohenschwangau Castle, where a music room had been placed at his disposal; in Munich, however, the newspaper *Der Volksbote* launched an attack on him and Wagner turned his venom on the leading Bavarian politicians in the *Neueste Nachrichten*, demanding their immediate dismissal and replacement. It was then that von der Pfordten wrote to the King and stated quite unequivocally that His Majesty must chose between the love and veneration of his people and his friendship with Richard Wagner. In a hastily convened meeting the cabinet threatened to resign if Wagner did not go, hinting that a revolution could well break out in Munich were such a dangerous troublemaker to remain. Not daring to risk an uprising and mindful of what had happened to his grandfather (who had been forced to abdicate after the scandalous affair with Lola Montez), Ludwig capitulated and wrote to Wagner demanding his extradition. After three days of fruitless haggling and pleading, Wagner took the train, alone, to Berne; Cosima did not return to her husband's house but to the house in the Brienner Strasse.

A fall from grace, then? All hopes, including those for a festival theatre with wide steps leading down to the river Isar, devoted solely to his work, dashed? No – Wagner's habitual resilience and tenacity came to the fore once again. Such a reversal in his fortunes must indeed have been dispiriting, but in the country house 'Les Artichauts' near Geneva he took up the orchestration of the last act of *Die Meistersinger*. He also convinced Ludwig that he was a royalist through and through and that only the princes could save Germany from the inevitable power struggle that must inexorably occur within the German *Bund* (Confederation). It may seem that he was dissembling by insisting on his loyalty to the idea of kingship,

Franz Hanfstaengl's photograph of Wagner taken in 1865.

given his earlier revolutionary activities (which were well known
to his opponents in Munich), but the idea of a popular monarch
at the head of a republic had always haunted him. But the plan for
his festival theatre? His initial enthusiasm for this had waned, for
he had always preferred the idea of building it in a small, provincial

Wagner's house in Tribschen, Switzerland.

town, far from centres of sophistication: a place where his admirers
would gather to be subject to *his* will alone, *his* vision and *his*
presence. Ludwig, meanwhile, toyed with the idea of abdication
and suicide; on 28 July he wrote to Wagner to say how much he
loved him, that he knelt before his bust in adoration, weeping
bitter tears. Wagner continued to work on *Die Meistersinger*;
Cosima joined him and they discovered on the Lake of Lucerne
the idyllic Haus Tribschen, which was to let. The King agreed to
pay the rent and it was here that Wagner and Cosima settled. And
it was also here that Wagner started dictating his autobiography
to Cosima and where, in many letters, he sought to deter the King

from abdicating: he may well have calculated that a king without power was of no use to him but he also believed that Bavaria, of all the principalities, could stand up to the overweening ambitions of Bismarck. On 22 May 1866, Wagner's 53rd birthday, a figure appeared at his doorstep dressed as a Franconian knight and announcing that he was Walther von Stolzing: it was Ludwig, together with an adjutant, Prince Paul von Taxis.[2] He returned to Munich two days later, where his subjects were appalled that he had gone incognito to this spendthrift degenerate in the face of mounting tensions vis-à-vis Prussian sabre-rattling.

But the King, increasingly unhappy and a stranger to reality, had the prospect of a war against Prussia before him, for Bavaria had thrown her lot in with Austria in an attempt to defy Prussia; he was also embroiled in an unsavoury scandal which was now unstoppable. To quash all rumours concerning his relationship with Cosima, Gräfin von Bülow, Wagner drew up a statement which the King had to sign insisting that this relationship was purely platonic and that von Bülow's honour was unimpeached; this statement would appear in the press. Ludwig dutifully signed it, sincerely believing in some metaphysical, spiritual relationship between himself, Wagner and Cosima, a holy trinity. Wagner, he believed in his more exalted moments, was a god who had descended from heaven in order to proclaim his new teaching and, in bringing joy to humanity, would redeem the world. It was inconceivable to him that Wagner could have stooped to promiscuity or lust: the stain of the world could never touch him.

But the world of politics could not be ignored: the Austrians were crushed at Königgrätz and within a week the Bavarians were defeated at Kissingen. Again, the King expressed the desire to abdicate but Cosima insisted that he remain, reminding him of the divine right of kings. On the same day, 24 July 1866, Wagner cast himself as Hans Sachs: just as Sachs was determined to prevent the elopement of Walther and Eva, so he, Wagner, advised

the King to leave 'monkish' Munich with its popish intrigues
and settle instead in Nuremberg, with its fresh Franconian air
and enlightened populace.

He was now deep in the composition sketches of the third act,
but suddenly fresh complications disturbed him. The deranged
Malwine Schnorr, bitterly envious of Cosima and hearing heavenly
voices which ordered her to marry Wagner, spread the rumour
at Court that Cosima and Wagner were lovers. It was then that
Ludwig, in ever increasing bewilderment, began to suspect his two
idols had deceived him. In January 1867 the surprise announcement
was made to a bemused Bavarian people that Ludwig II had become
engaged to his cousin Sophie Charlotte ('Parzival bridegroom'
Wagner noted in his diary); this engagement would last less than a
year. In February Cosima gave birth to Wagner's second daughter,
Eva; her husband, at her bedside, said '*Je pardonne*', to which his
wife replied '*Il ne faut pas pardonner, il faut comprendre.*' Wagner
put the finishing touches to *Die Meistersinger*; the King graciously
received him in Munich and, despite the tensions between them
(and there were others: disagreement on whether or not the aging
Tichatschek should sing the role of the radiant *Lohengrin*; Wagner's
articles on German art and politics and his criticism of Frederick the
Great for his contempt for all things German), arrangements were
made to stage Wagner's glorification of Nuremberg. The premiere
took place in Munich on 21 June 1868; it was Wagner's greatest
success since *Rienzi* and, during the prelude he was summoned
to Ludwig's royal box where, after each act, he stood to receive
the jubilant ovations. An unprecedented breach of etiquette?
Indeed, but the King could bask in the waves of adulation which
his beloved received.

Die Meistersinger von Nürnberg is held by many to be Wagner's
greatest work, from the glorious C major chords of the overture,
through its consummate orchestration, to its richness of detail and
its predominant diatonicism. Astonishing too is the fusion of old

and new, the re-creation of sixteenth-century Nuremberg and the homage to J. S. Bach in the use of chorales, counterpoint and fugal structures. Much later in his mental life, even after his apostasy, Nietzsche would give in the eighth chapter of *Beyond Good and Evil* the finest description ever written of the overture to Wagner' drama; he heard, he wrote,

> once again for the first time, Wagner's prelude, a piece of magnificent, gorgeous, heavy, latter-day art which has the pride to presuppose two centuries of music as still living in order that it may be understood: – it is an honour to the Germans that such a pride is not out of place![3]

It seemed to many that Wagner had now left the world of myth and legend and returned to history; he had studied the sources carefully and knew the dramatic poem *Hans Sachs* by Ludwig Deinhardstein, as well as Lortzing's opera, which is based on it (1840; revised 1845). An invocation of Nuremberg, then, at the

Stage set by Josef Hoffmann for the Festival Meadow (Act Three) of *Die Meistersinger von Nürnberg* (1862–7).

height of its fame, and of the poet and shoemaker Hans Sachs?
A portrayal of the guilds, the customs, the festivals? Apparently,
but Wagner in fact gives us an image of Nuremberg as filtered
through the Romanticism of Ludwig Tieck (whom he had met in
1847 to discuss *Lohengrin* inter alia) and Wilhelm Wackenroder,
whose joint *Herzensergiessungen eines kunstliebenden Klosterbruders*
(Effusions of an Art-loving Brother, 1797) had contained portrayals
of Albrecht Dürer as well as an extremely fanciful description of
the city, a city where, in actual fact, the craftsmen were not organized into guilds but remained under the strict control of the town
council. There was no festival meadow and certainly no procession
like the one Wagner gives us in Act Three. Wagner provides an
aestheticized Nuremberg: he had not 'returned to history' but
bathed the city in a golden glow of incomparable music, a 'stream
of delight', in Nietzsche's terms, 'of old and new happiness',
including especially the joy of the artist in himself, which he
refuses to conceal, his 'astonished, happy cognizance of his
mastery'. Did Wagner portray his earlier tempestuous self in
Walther von Stolzing? Perhaps, but he also portrays himself as
Hans Sachs, who knows that genius must also respect the best
in tradition: Wagner, baptized in St Thomas's Church, Leipzig,
admires the greatness of Bach and also delights in the Italianate
tradition – which Mozart also used – of mistaken identities,
cloaked figures, a serenade beneath the window and the rest.

Sachs, the world-weary cobbler, seeks to direct untrammelled
Dionysian outpourings into a master-song; he also seeks to restrain
the violent outpouring of energy (the riot at the end of Act Two)
and channel it into a more controllable, more structured course.
This is the meaning of his great '*Wahn*' monologue, '*Wahn*' being
best understood as illusion or madness, and the people's unre-
strained emotions must be transmuted into something more
constructive: that is, participation in the song contest as judges.
On a more personal level, Sachs wisely sees that his love for Eva

'The Acclamation of Hans Sachs', from *Die Meistersinger von Nürnberg*, a postcard reproduction after a painting by Franz Stassen.

(of which she is well aware and naughtily reciprocates) must be overcome; he does not wish to have the role of King Marke (Isolde's deluded husband) foisted upon him – and how poignantly the *Tristan* chord is heard in the orchestra. He seeks for order suffused with humanity; he is greeted rapturously by the people as a manifestion of the popular spirit and in the tremendous chorus '*Wach auf!*' (Awake!), hailed by them in the words of the Reformation. The young knight, under his tutelage, wins the contest and the hand of Eva; he is also put firmly in his place by Sachs when he refuses to be accepted as a 'Meister'. German art, and the traditions from which it sprang, must be honoured: then all will be well.

A word on the hapless Beckmesser. As town clerk he holds a position of some standing and as marker of the guild he is respected as a figure of authority. But he also becomes the stock figure of derision found in many operas – the ageing bachelor who decides to compete for the hand of a young girl. This will prove his undoing as he steals what he believes to be Sachs's song and becomes a grotesque and pitiable figure of fun. Difficulties arise in any attempt to see him as a Jew (an absurd notion in sixteenth-century Nuremberg) or as someone somehow betraying Semitic qualities.[4] Recent scholarship by Barry Millington has also argued that he may be linked to the victim in Grimm's story *Der Jude im Dorn* (The Jew in the Thornbush),[5] but skilful and very plausible counter-arguments have been put forward. Sixtus Beckmesser is cleverly drawn as a pedant – and a typically German pedant, interested only in the 'rules', a narrow-minded functionary with no sense of beauty. After being soundly trounced in the contest, he rejoins the people ('*verliert sich unter dem Volke*') and presumably puts his unseemly desire for the young girl (and her money?) behind him.

Hans Sachs's final words (which, incidentally, Wagner had considered expunging, preferring the Prize Song to be the climax until Cosima insisted on their retention) have given rise to much speculation. He warns of dark times to come (the Thirty Years War?), also a time (absolutism) when princes do not understand their people, preferring instead to ape foreign habits and customs, ignoring what is genuine and indulging in falsehood and trumpery (Wagner's criticism of Frederick the Great of Prussia for constantly speaking French and showing very little interest in German culture may be seen here). It is German *art* which is paramount, and even if the Holy Roman Empire should crumble to dust (as it would in 1806), then Germany's contribution to world culture will prevail. With this ringing proclamation Wagner's radiant masterpiece comes to its triumphant conclusion.

Friedrich Nietzsche was one of the most fascinating figures to fall under Wagner's spell. They first met in Leipzig at the home of Wagner's brother-in-law Hermann Brockhaus, when Nietzsche was 24 and Wagner 31 years his senior; Nietzsche later gave a very amusing portrayal of the composer. He was 'a fabulously passionate man who spoke very quickly, was very witty and was the life and soul of our small, very private gathering'.[6] Before and after dinner he played the most important passages of *Die Meistersinger* at the piano, imitating all the voices, and was extremely boisterous; he also read sections of his autobiography relating to his days as a student in Leipzig. He was very impressed by Nietzsche's knowledge of his music and invited him to visit him in Tribschen: this Nietzsche would do, very frequently, when he had the chair of classical philology at Basel. (Nietzsche would later, after his mental collapse, speak of himself as Dionysus, Wagner as the Minotaur and Cosima as Ariadne, whom he loved.) Cosima, after the success of *Die Meistersinger*, finally and irrevocably, moved into Tribschen with her daughters Isolde and Eva; she was now pregnant with Wagner's third child. She would there start to keep her diary of her life with Wagner, which she would write until his death in Venice in February 1883.

Wagner now set about returning to the massive *Ring* material. He was pleased to hear that the King desired a new production of *Tristan und Isolde* but annoyed at His Majesty's demand to see *Das Rheingold* performed in Munich. The King, as lawful owner of the score, had every right to do so, but Wagner refused, insisting that the four parts *must* be performed together, not piecemeal. The birth of his son Siegfried on 6 June 1869 (Nietzsche was, apparently, in the house and blissfully unaware of what was going on) gave him great joy, which is surely reflected in the jubilant rapture at the end of *Siegfried*; he also received visits from French admirers, including Catulle Mendès, Villiers de l'Isle-Adam and Judith Gautier, who, however, insisted on travelling to Munich for the rehearsals of *Das Rheingold*. On hearing of these rehearsals Wagner demanded that Hans Richter the conductor and Franz Betz (Wotan) withdraw; the King, furious, damned Wagner and his cohorts. Travelling to Munich, Wagner attempted to sabotage the planned production, risking the King's wrath even further; on returning to Tribschen he threatened the conductor Franz Wüllner with the following words:

Hands off my score! Take my advice, Sir, or may the devil take you! . . . I am going to teach the pair of you [Wüllner and the theatre manager Baron Karl von Perfall] a lot of lessons before you learn how ignorant you are.[7]

The premiere took place on 22 September, in Wagner's absence; two weeks later he began work on the Norns' scene for *Götter-dämerung*. In the spring of 1870 he informed the King that he was immersed in this work; the outer world had no interest for him. He ignored the fact that the Berlin premiere of *Die Meistersinger* was not a success, and that *Die Walküre* had been successfully staged in Munich, despite his having bluntly asked the King on 20 November 1869, 'Do you want my work as I want it? Or some wretched operatic repertory for subscribers and critics?' In the summer of 1870, *Das*

Rheingold and *Die Walküre* were performed three times in Munich and Brahms, Liszt and the violinist Joachim all attended; Wagner, in Tribschen, discussed Greek tragedy with Professor Nietzsche, who now had a room set aside for his personal use, and insolently ignored any world which was not of his making.

The outer world did impinge, however, in the form of the Franco–Prussian war. Certain French friends were naturally ill at ease but Saint-Saëns accompanied Wagner on the piano during the latter's declamation of certain passages of the *Ring*. Work was also started on Wagner's essay 'Beethoven', commemorating the centenary of the musician's birth. This essay is about Schopenhauer (and Wagner) as well as Beethoven, and insists that it is the *musician* who is able to express the ultimate truth of things; ignoring the specious glitter of transient phenomena, the listener turns away from appearance and attains a state which is akin to trance. The musician, we learn, 'dews the brain' with his wonder drops of sound (IX, p. 53) and robs it of the power of seeing anything save our own inner world. Music expresses an inner vision: life and death, the whole import and existence of the outer world, hang on nothing but the innermost movement of the soul, and the purely extrinsic is relegated to a penumbrous existence. Turning to Beethoven, Wagner describes the state of ecstasy called forth in a musician such as Beethoven when he saw through specious reality to the ultimate itself: inspiration overwhelmed him and he knew that he had seen through the turmoil of life and gained the wisdom that only a saint achieved in beatitude (IX, p. 71). Wagner's old adversary Eduard Hanslick, writing in the Viennese *Neue freie Presse* in 1870, was not impressed by the essay, finding Wagner's assertion that music should enfold drama entirely within itself and that drama should express only an idea of the world adequate to music meaningless: this was special pleading on Wagner's part to justify his own concept of music drama, the artwork of the future. Shakespeare's drama, Wagner seemed to believe, finds its counterpart only in Beethoven's music. And the identity of Shakespearean and Beethovian drama? This can only be the work, Hanslick muses, of a great poet-musician, one who is a Shakespeare and a Beethoven at once. He does not tell us who this phenomenon might be but knew that it would not be beyond the wit of his readers to guess.[8]

Wagner's wife had died on the morning of 25 January 1866; on 25 August 1870 he and Cosima (now divorced) were married in the Protestant church in Lucerne, with Hans Richter and Malwida von Meysenbug as witnesses. The newly married couple delighted in the Prussian victories over the French, and Cosima's diaries will bear witness to this. The Wagners were indeed caught up in the jingoism which was sweeping through Germany; the French were crushingly defeated at Sedan on 2 September when Napoleon III and his army surrendered. Some two months later Wagner penned a farce, a so-called 'comedy in the antique manner' entitled *Eine Kapitulation* under the pseudonym of Aristop Hanes; this is generally rejected (particularly by those who have not read it) as a boorish piece of tasteless chauvinism exulting in the tribulations of the humiliated Parisians. A closer examination, however (and it should be remembered that Paris did not actually capitulate until 28 January 1871), shows that the capitulation in question is that of the Germans before French light opera. This is what Gambetta claims in the farce, and towards the end Jacques Offenbach appears, founder of the modern operetta and a German to boot, born in Cologne. According to Wagner, it is the Prussians who had sent Offenbach as a negotiator. The ladies of the ballet appear, as does Victor Hugo, the 'genius of France', announcing that the Germans can now be given all they require: 'Chignons and pomades/And shows and promenades/*concert populaire*/there's all you've wanted there!'[9] This farce is indeed a curiosity, but Wagner published it in his collected works in 1873: the Parisians may well have been shelled and battered by Prussian bombardment but the blandishments of the belle époque (in which a German – Offenbach – had played an important part) were, it seems, irresistible.

The year ended with the first volume of *My Life* (the young Professor Nietzsche had read and corrected the proofs), and on Christmas Day a little concert was given in the stairwell at Tribschen, the *Siegfried Idyll*, played by a band of fifteen players conducted by Wagner himself. It was meant as a birthday present for Cosima – whose birthday was, in fact, on 24 December but she preferred the more prestigious date of the next day – and a token of gratitude for the birth of a son.

The years between 1871 and 1876 brought momentous changes to Wagner's life: the move to Bayreuth, the completion of the *Ring* cycle, regarded by some to be one of the cornerstones of Western culture, the building against colossal odds of his own Festspielhaus and the subsequent performances there in the presence of two emperors, two kings, sundry princes and some of the leading composers of the day. His boast that this was the first time in the history of artistic creativity that royalty came at the artist's behest and not he to theirs is justified; his ruthless ambition, absolute belief in his own genius, strength of will and almost superhuman energy had triumphed.

After the German victory over France, Wagner sought to ingratiate himself with the new Prussian state, sensing that Ludwig's status was rapidly diminishing. He proposed a 'Funeral Symphony for the Fallen' and a festive march with massed choruses but the Prussian government turned this down, reminding him tartly that he did not have a monopoly on the national spirit; a '*Kaisermarsch*' was, however, composed, intended as a march for the imperial coronation or even as the source of a national anthem. With Cosima he visited Bayreuth to inspect the Markgräfliches Opernhaus, an exquisite eighteenth-century theatre built by the Markgräfin Wilhelmine, sister of

Cosima and Wagner photographed by Fritz Luckhardt in May 1872.

Frederick the Great; it was obvious, however, that this Rococo jewel was totally inappropriate for his purposes. But the town pleased him for reasons that were also political. It was in Bavaria (whose king, despite everything, was still pining for him) but it also had been a possession of the Hohenzollerns – Prussian, therefore – and Wagner was keen to demonstrate his current admiration for those now in power. Later, in May, he announced in Leipzig that the first Festival would take place in 1873, and continued work on *Götterdämmerung*.

In the following year, 1872, he obtained a plot of land on which to build his villa, now the Hofgarten: Ludwig was to provide 25,000 thalers towards the cost. The site for a new theatre was finally settled, just outside the town on a slight rise, and preparations were made to vacate Tribschen. The move affected Nietzsche deeply; he had visited the house on the lake 23 times and somehow sensed (correctly) that things would never be the same again between him and Wagner. On Wagner's birthday, at eleven in the morning, in pouring rain, the foundation stone was laid; at five in the afternoon, in the old opera house, a performance of Beethoven's Ninth Symphony was given; at seven there was a banquet in the Hotel Sonne. Wagner now threw himself wholeheartedly into conducting, raising money and looking for singers as well as attempting to complete the last, most daunting part of his tetralogy; hopes for a Festival in 1873 were now rapidly fading.

At the beginning of 1874 Wagner desperately sought to persuade the Grand Duke of Baden to intervene on his behalf with the Emperor to secure 125,000 thalers for the complete *Ring* to be performed in 1876 as a commemoration of the peace treaty with France in 1871; the Grand Duke, on studying the details, withdrew his support. In desperation Wagner turned once more to King Ludwig; on 6 January he heard from Lorenz von Düfflipp, Ludwig's Court secretary, that Ludwig could not underwrite the Bayreuth Festival and that consequently the whole project was in jeopardy.

Wagner's letter of 9 January is a masterpiece of cunning. He felt constrained, he wrote, that in consequence of certain machinations he had had to abandon the projected performance of the *Ring*; he would also have to content himself with having built a theatre knowing full well that any performances staged there would lose all significance since they were incapable of arousing further interest from 'my royal benefactor for whose fame and enjoyment I had chiefly desired to summon them into existence'.[10] He was adopting the right tone and he knew it. On 25 January the reply came from the King, who promised to stand security for a loan.

> No, no, and *no* again! It should not end like this. Help must be forthcoming! Our plan must not fail. Parzival knows his calling and will do all that it lies in his power to do.[11]

This 'poor fool' had averted disaster, and Wagner's cunningly obsequious letter of gratitude may well be imagined.

He put the finishing touches to the orchestral score of Act Three of *Götterdämmerung*, and consequently of the whole tetralogy, on Saturday 21 November: he had started the poems, we recall, in October 1848, the music in November 1853. He had scarcely been daunted by the immensity of the scale; he had completed it despite enormous difficulties; he had laid the foundation stone of his own theatre with its auditorium shaped as an amphitheatre, its double proscenium and its hidden orchestra. Act Three of *Siegfried* had brought the young hero to the breasts and lips of a woman who had once been a Valkyrie; their ecstatic union showed how love triumphs and how malevolence (Mime) and flickering fire are overcome. It is amazing indeed that Wagner could pick up the leitmotifs he had used years before, and modify them, and the immensely richer orchestration of *Siegfried*'s third act, the vast and varied orchestral resources which he developed, are abundantly evident in *Götterdämmerung*, this climactic work.

And the difficulties facing him *were* prodigious: he had to return to a libretto written over twenty years earlier and look back at the music – an abundance of leitmotifs which now, after *Tristan und Isolde* and *Die Meistersinger von Nürnberg*, must have seemed woefully underdeveloped. *Siegfried*'s third act had demonstrated a tremendous advance on the earlier two dramas that preceded it; now he could move forward to *Götterdämmerung* and demonstrate an incomparable weight and sonority of orchestration, a prodigious modification of earlier leitmotifs, a gorgeous fabric of sound.

The main difficulty facing Wagner was the abandonment of his earliest socialist-utopian views: *Götterdämmerung* does not portray a transfigured world where free love prevails, but a world of deception, cunning, violence and murder which, together with Valhalla, is ripe for destruction. Is it a reversal to grand opera, as Shaw has argued?[12] It should be remembered that the prose draft of *Siegfrieds Tod* dates from 1848, merely six years after *Rienzi*'s premiere in Dresden; Wagner also left far behind him the self-imposed strictures of his earlier Zurich writings, which had set down rules to which only *Das Rheingold* had adhered. *Götterdämmerung*, with its blood-brotherhood oaths, its magic draught, its swearing of vengeance which outdoes even Verdi, its massed chorus of vassals, its shattering funeral music, its scenes of immolation and *Ragnarök*, was surely Wagner's greatest achievement to date, musically and theatrically. Not only did he take up the gargantuan *Ring* material again: he drove it forward to a tremendous conclusion. And he was more than equal to the task, fusing myth with psychology and poetic drama worthy of the Greeks with the symphonic music of a Beethoven. But *Ragnarök* is perhaps the wrong word: it is not the world which is destroyed but Valhalla and the hall of the Gibichungs, both defiled and corrupt. A handful of spectators watches this, and life will somehow continue, as the director Joachim Herz rightly saw:

Hope has been born . . . its seed will burgeon, as is clear from the violin melody that Wagner has held back for this very moment. It is the melody with which Sieglinde had expressed her joy on hearing that new life was stirring within her, the fruit of an unlawful love, an ecstatic joy that also includes gratitude at the courageous help of one person for another, of one woman for another. And now these sounds proclaim that a new world might be a better one.[13]

And finally to Brünnhilde's self-immolation. Having learned from the Rhinemaidens that it was Alberich's demonic lust for power, the determination to return the ring to his father Hagen, which enmeshed Siegfried in an evil plot aimed at alienating him from his wife in order that Hagen might learn from her where her husband's weak spot could be found in her desire for vengeance, Brünnhilde now knows that the corrupt court of the Gibichungs must be destroyed and Valhalla with it; she will die with her

The Bühnen-Festspielhaus, Bayreuth, c. 1905.

husband in an act of redemptive catharsis while the ring is returned to the waters.

The Festspielhaus was completed in the summer of 1875 and rehearsals began shortly afterwards. Wagner insisted on being everywhere, and it is of interest that he demanded that one Richard Fricke, a maître de ballet, should help him. Fricke obeyed and followed Wagner's order that the complicated swimming of the Rhinemaidens should be done choreographically (Wagner's essay 'Über das Dirigieren' [On Conducting, 1869] had also stressed the importance of the Ballettmeister who determines how everything should move, how the tempo should be kept, stressing the ensemble above all). Wagner was constantly on the stage, acting, demonstrating, remonstrating. To earn money he agreed, in February 1876, to write an American Centennial March, commissioned by Philadelphia for the generous fee of $5,000; in the following month he could not resist rehearsing *Tristan und Isolde* for its Berlin premiere and was received during the interval by the Emperor, who pledged financial support; in the same month he conducted *Lohengrin* in Vienna at a benefit performance and was greeted at the railway station waiting room by a massive chorus singing '*Wach auf!*' from *Die Meistersinger*. The atmosphere in Bayreuth became increasingly febrile as August approached. Wagner received from Nietzsche a copy of the latter's *Thoughts out of Season*, a collection of essays, the fourth of which was entitled 'Richard Wagner in Bayreuth'; Wagner scarcely had time to read it and simply congratulated the young man on his knowledge of the composer ('Friend, your book is tremendous! How on earth did you learn so much about me?!'). This essay is certainly laudatory in tone, but a certain reserve is also present. The Wagner of Bayreuth was not quite the same as the Wagner Nietzsche had met in 1868 and the Wagner of Tribschen who had fascinated him. Nietzsche found the atmosphere of Bayreuth increasingly uncongenial; it seemed that Wagner had lost an earlier idealism and was becoming increasingly worldly in his ambitions. The halcyon days were gone forever and the professor of classical philology became increasingly prone to headaches and bouts of sickness (caused, Wagner would tactlessly speculate in a letter to Otto Eiser, Nietzsche's doctor, by excessive masturbation[14]) which made him avoid the frenetically charged atmosphere of the town. He was invited to the rehearsals and arrived on 24 July, in sombre mood; despite his migraines he attended *Götterdämmerung,* also *Das Rheingold* and *Die Walküre*. His eyesight deteriorated and, some time before the dress rehearsals he fled to Klingenbrunn in the Bavarian Forest. And the king who had, despite everything, helped immeasurably? Ludwig II arrived by night in a private train from which he descended at a signal box outside the town to avoid the inevitable adulation. He attended four dress rehearsals and then, at night, departed for Hohenschwangau. He did not experience the arrival of the German Emperor Wilhelm I, who, on meeting Wagner at the railway station declared: 'I did not believe you would ever do it.' (x, p. 51)

But he had. He had created, in a gigantic eruption of talent and genius, a musical-dramatic world, a tretralogy unequalled in the history of art. The mystic grandeur of these works, as Roger Scruton has written, overwhelm the listener by their fusion of thinking and feeling; they take forward the inner language forged by Beethoven and give Western civilization its last experience of the *heroic*.[15] They are inspired visions of human suffering and love, transcending banal reality and climax in cleansing fire and lustral water. Thomas Mann wrote on the *Ring*'s epic radicalism, its portrayal of the mythic archetypes of man; it is a work which touches on some of the most basic instincts and passions of human nature through the sensual medium of incomparable music.[16]

An atavistic work? A fairy tale? What is without doubt is the enthusiasm engendered by the *Ring*, the sense of grandeur which seizes the listener on hearing it is comparable only to the feelings inspired by nature at its noblest. Its sheer size and complexity mean that this is a work existing on many levels; Wagner has, dexterously, welded together the myth of the gods, the drama of the Wälsung siblings (Siegmund and Sieglinde), the tale of the young man setting forth to slay a dragon and the tragedy of this man's later enmeshment in sinister machinations and Brünnhilde's revenge. Wagner achieved all this by his leitmotivic techniques and succeeded, as Carl Dahlhaus has described, 'through the magic power of metaphor and allegory to draw the listener into a world of musico-poetic relationships where, in the end, everything seems to belong to everything else'.[17]

One final word on *Götterdämmerung*'s last pages and meanings. Wagner worked on various possibilities: one ending would have had Brünnhilde, before thrusting a burning brand into Siegfried's funeral pyre, declaring that love was more precious than goods or gold. Wagner rejected this as sounding too trite, as he also rejected another possible ending full of Schopenhauerian-Buddistic images ('redemption from world-wandering, from reincarnation', flight from 'the world of delusion' and so on) and finishing with the utterance 'I saw the world end.' He left the ending as we have it now, knowing that the orchestra tells us all that we need to know. Joachim Herz has described this; the tentative watchers of the destruction will, it is hoped, inherit a world purged of violence and greed. It will be a world without gods but where human love could again prevail. This the young revolutionary had hoped for in 1848 and this he now presented to the world for emperors, kings and princes to understand.

Three cycles of the *Ring* were given (on 13–17, 20–23 and 27–30 August), the last attended by Ludwig; during a celebratory banquet Wagner embraced Liszt, declaring that without him none of this, Wagner's vision, would have been realized: the Festival *had* taken place. But dark thoughts also assailed him and, on 7 September, he wrote to Lili Lehmann (Woglinde) that 'there was so much that we shall have to put right next year'.[18] He had been warned by Richard Fricke and also Karl Brandt, who had designed all the Bayreuth machines, not to demand excessive explicitness: would the dragon not appear ludicrous? (It was not the fault of Wagner, however, that the British firm had misdirected the dragon's neck and sent it elsewhere.) He had also become increasingly unsettled when the designers unwillingly tried to realize his written prescriptions. The gas lighting for the auditorium had only been installed a few hours before *Das Rheingold* was due to begin and had not functioned properly. The rehearsals had gone well but the opening night was reminiscent of a provincial theatre with a backdrop hastily raised to reveal workmen in shirtsleeves. After the performance Wagner refused to appear and sat fuming in his room, cursing all the singers except Karl Hill (Alberich); he was furious with the costumes, with Hans Richter's tempi . . . He was also soon to learn that there had been a catastrophic deficit of 48,000 marks. Exhausted and suffering from an inevitable feeling of anticlimax, Wagner found relief in a love affair with Judith Gautier, now divorced from Catulle Mendès. It was she who would later provide for him perfumes and silks from Paris when he was working on *Parsifal*.

In his blackest moments, Wagner wondered whether his work had any future in the new Germany. The press was inimical: in Vienna the critic Ludwig Speidel called the *Ring* an '*Affenschande*' ('crying shame') which had nothing to do with the German people, who should, if they ever find pleasure in such a work, be removed from the ranks of the cultured peoples of Western Europe. Other critics described the tetralogy as a hotchpotch, a madness, a brutality. The Wagners travelled abroad to Sorrento to escape and stayed a month in the Hotel Victoria; by chance Nietzsche was also in Sorrento, staying with Malwida von Meysen-bug, and he and Wagner met for the last time. Nietzsche saw that his erstwhile mentor, friend and master was already drawing away from the world of the *Ring* and moving towards more recondite, transcendental realms. Wagner had shown his contemporaries what the power of his will had achieved and demonstrated the total emotional submission that his music demanded. To quote William Blisset's startling assertion, 'He had entered world history; he must enter sacred history.'[19] How 'sacred' his final preoccupation was will be examined in the next chapter.

6

Consummation

'Et, ô ces voix d'enfants chantant dans la coupole!'

Parsifal (or, rather, Parzifal, this being Wagner's original spelling[1])
had, in a sense, never left him since that remarkable summer of
1845 in Marienbad, where he had read the Middle High German
poem (we recall that he had also planned, in his original sketch
for a three-act opera on Tristan and Isolde, that Parsifal, on his
wanderings, should visit Tristan's sick bed, but this was later
dropped.) When moving into the Wesendonck's summer house,
the 'Asyl', in 1857 he also described waking on Good Friday to
beautiful spring weather and birdsong, and remembering how
meaningful this had been in Wolfram's masterpiece:[2] this may
have been a slip of memory or poetic licence as Good Friday was
on 10 April that year and the Wagners moved into the house on
28 April. Most interesting is a letter to Mathilde of early August
1860 in which Wagner narrated the new version of *Tannhäuser*
and the prose translations of his first mature pieces (*Der fliegende
Holländer, Tannhäuser, Lohengrin* and *Tristan*) which would soon
be published, and emphasized how deeply he had been affected by
Lohengrin's story; this was the most tragic of the first four dramas.
He enunciated the concept of metempsychosis and, in Buddhistic
terms, sees the 'spotless beauty of Lohengrin as explicable in terms
of his being a continuation of Parsifal'. Elsa would reach this level
by also being reborn (she, Savitri, 'reaches the love of Ananda').

Wagner then turned his attention to *Tristan und Isolde* which was, and would ever be, a miracle to him. How terribly, he wrote, would he have to atone for this work one day. Then follow long descriptions of *Parsifal*: one day, he explained, when everything else has matured within him, it would be an unprecedented pleasure to complete this poem.[3] It is Kundry whom he now describes in considerable detail, although she is yet unnamed, and Mathilde is teasingly asked to identify her. Most important is also the prose sketch of 1865 which the King had requested and which Wagner provided and dispatched to Hohenschwangau on 31 August; a week later the King, ecstatic, thanked him and assured his adored, holy friend of his undying love.

Parsifal, which would take him some seventeen years to complete, may be seen as a work of summation. Kundry is, to some extent, anticipated by Venus and Klingsor's magic garden by the Venusberg while Monsalvat is foreshadowed by that transcendental realm from which Lohengrin, son of Parsifal, descends. In *Lohengrin* a question is asked which should not have been, and in *Parsifal* a question should have been asked which was not. We also see something of Alberich, who foreswore love and sought world domination in Klingsor, and Parsifal's dallying with the flower-maidens is reminiscent of Siegfried's teasing the Rhine-maidens. Parsifal, the pure fool brought up in the wilderness and called upon to be the saviour of the world he knows nothing about, is a Siegfried figure, for Kundry tells us in Act One that he once conquered villains and giants who feared the mettlesome boy.[4] He also, like Siegfried, may have had an erotic mother complex and had presumably led the life of an unthinking hobbledehoy until the incident with the swan and Gurnemanz's reprimand. It is the figure of Amfortas who relates most clearly to another wounded hero – Tristan: this Wagner explored in an earlier letter to Mathilde of 30 May 1859. He was working, he wrote, on the third act of the work (*Tristan und Isolde*) where the most unprecedented suffering

Rogelio Egusquiza, 'The Holy Grail' from *Parsifal*, 1893, etching, aquatint and drypoint.

and yearning are portrayed – and he then realized that it was Amfortas who springs vividly to mind.[5] His agony was that of his third-act Tristan inconceivably intensified. This wretched man, Wagner explained, knows of no other longing in his terrible pain than the longing to die: he demands to be allowed a glimpse of the Grail in the hope that this might at least close his wounds (for everything else is useless – nothing can help him). But the Grail can only show him that he *cannot* die (both Tristan and Amfortas in Wagner's completed dramas tear open their bandages from their suppurating wounds, allowing their tormented blood to spurt forth). *Parsifal* was, then, the inevitable climax to Wagner's life and work and with the *Ring* behind him he was able to complete the poem *Parsifal* (one of his shortest) which he read aloud to Cosima. Now in his 64th year, with the strains of setting up the Bayreuth venture increasingly apparent, and the empty Festspiel-haus standing on the hill as a constant rebuke (or, in his darkest moments, an all-too tangible token of monumental folly), he sensed that *Parsifal* would be his crowning achievement, a work to be performed only in Bayreuth and not on vulgar stages defiled by meretricious inanities. The work would also *consecrate* the stage: it would be a '*Bühnenweihfestspiel*', a clumsy word which may be translated as a 'sacred stage festival play' and which demonstrates how seriously he took the task in hand. He had, before it was built, described it in a letter to the King on 11 August 1873 as a Castle of the Grail, devoted to art and far removed from the common manifestations of human activity, a Monsalvat where sacerdotal rites of purification and regeneration may be experi-enced, accessible only to those initiated into its mysteries. It was now time to turn this vision into reality.

Yet in 1877 vulgar reality asserted itself, as it had in 1855, in the need to pay off enormous debts (something in the region of 100,000 marks). Wagner was forced to accept an invitation from the Old Philharmonic Society in London to conduct a series of concerts in the newly built Albert Hall. In contrast to the ill-fated visit of 1855, Wagner was now known throughout Europe and America; he was no longer seen as a disreputable outsider but as a musician who had accomplished amazing if daunting, even incomprehensible, artistic feats. The Albert Hall concerts were designed to outline his operatic development from *Rienzi* to the

Ring, with three of his marches included; pieces from *Tristan und Isolde* were also permitted. The Albert Hall was filled with glorious sound and, despite some carping criticism, the reviews were generally enthusiastic: even the vinegary Davison of *The Times*, hitherto unimpressed by Wagner, admitted that the duet from the second act of *Tristan* contained music of supreme beauty. The last scheduled concert was a triumph: 'Proceeds of £1,600 and a very animated audience' Cosima reported in her diary on 19 May 1877, 'very un-English we are told, R. crowned with a laurel wreath and unending cheers.' There were meetings with Robert Browning and George Eliot and G. H. Lewes, and Cosima sat for Burne-Jones. There was an audience at Windsor with Queen Victoria and her son Prince Leopold; that same evening, 17 May, Wagner read his *Parsifal* to a select gathering. But despite the success of the last evening, the financial result of the visit was a bitter disappointment. His agents, Hodge and Essex, were on the point of bankruptcy, having foolishly been ignorant of the fact that one-third of the seats in the Albert Hall were privately owned and not available for public use. Wagner's despairing words as the train pulled out of Victoria Station on 4 June were purported to have been '*Alles verloren, nur die Ehre nicht*' (All is lost, except honour); after paying some of his musicians and singers out of his own pocket, he had earned £700.[6]

On his return he worked at *Parsifal* and also hoped that his idea of a music academy to teach conductors and singers to excel in model performances of his works would come to fruition. He had felt keen disappointment at the poor artistic standards of the Festival of 1876 and groaned at the idea of staging *Parsifal* within the inadequacies and restrictions of the theatrical techniques of his day. The thought of his most fascinating creation – Kundry – being made up as a late Victorian *femme fatale* gave him much displeasure. He had, he boasted, created the invisible orchestra and now he sought to invent an 'invisible theatre'. He also slyly suggested that Kundry should lie in her bower naked as a Venus by Titian (to Cosima 23 December 1878). In his new music school he would show the world what *could* be done with new productions of *Der fliegende Holländer, Tannhäuser* and *Lohengrin*. But nothing came of the idea and he turned instead to the *Bayreuther Blätter*, a house journal which was to survive from 1878 to 1938 under the editorship of Hans von Wolzogen. Wagner instigated it: it was intended as a mouthpiece for members of the Bayreuth circle to disseminate his ideas on art and life (he had originally considered collaborating on the journal with Nietzsche: this obviously came to nothing). But these *Blätter* came to be associated with extreme forms of German nationalism, and it must be made quite clear that Wagner very quickly sought to have very little to do with them.

As early as autumn 1876, a letter to Wolzogen expressed a feeling of resignation on Wagner's part; on 16 December 1880 Cosima's diary gives ample evidence of Wagner's growing disillusionment ('Richard sees his thoughts caricatured in the journal'). Already on 19 September of that year, when the conversation turned to Wolzogen and the *Blätter*, Wagner referred to the journal as a 'spectre' from which he distanced himself. On 22 February 1882 he was 'in an extremely bad mood' when reading a supplement to the *Blätter*; on 9 February 1883 he was in a very black mood and spoke disparagingly about his supporters who seemed bent on reducing his ideas to absurdity: he never believed for one moment that the *Blätter* would last for two years (he even went as far as to regret he had ever built Wahnfried: the Festivals also seemed absurd!).[7] To equate Wagner, then, with the wayward, and even grotesque views put forward in this journal is therefore erroneous; he did not set the points for the maunderings of a writer like Houston Stewart Chamberlain, who was later to marry his daughter Eva and, in 1923, greet Hitler as a man destined to save Germany from defeat and humiliation. Hanslick, with no scholarly analysis,

Franz von Lenbach, *Cosima Wagner*, 1879, oil on canvas.

referred to the 'Richard Wagner cult', a deification of the composer
with his own knowledge and consent; Max Nordau, in typically
manic, entertaining and journalistic fashion, portrayed the *Blätter*
as a unique phenomenon, explaining that

> no other instance is known of a newspaper which was founded
> exclusively for the deification of a living man, in every number

of which, through long years, the appointed priests of the temple have burned incense to the household god, with the savage fanaticism of howling and dancing dervishes, bent the knee, prostrated themselves before him and immolated all opponents as sacrificial victims.[8]

Wagner had the good sense to distance himself from it; he certainly published *Kunst und Religion* (Art and Religion) in it together with its supplements, also a scattering of essays, many of which continued his earlier criticism of society deriving from his Zurich days; it must be understood, however, that in opposing many aspects of contemporary society he was showing his opposition to the new German *Reich* and would never have been able to agree with these members of the Bayreuth circle who insisted on seeing the fall and redemption of Monsalvat as a symbol of Germany awaiting *her* redeemer. Wagner never thought within these narrow nationalistic parameters: time and again he despaired of living in Germany, where he was misunderstood or, worse, ignored, and he often toyed with the idea of moving to America. A most enlightening letter is the one written from Naples on 8 February 1880 to Newell Sill Jenkins, an American dentist practising in Dresden.[9] Wagner explained that his patience would soon run out with regard to his hopes for Germany and her future and that he may yet decide to emigrate to America with his family. He would need a lump sum of $1 million, half of which would pay for his settlement in 'a climatically beneficial State of the Union', the rest being deposited 'in a state bank as a capital investment at five per cent'. In exchange, America would secure his services for all time: he would present all his works for model performances there, beginning – surprisingly – with *Parsifal*. He also reminds the dentist that he had kindly offered to arrange a concert tour, but Wagner is now adamant that he had no intention of touring and returning. 'Only a complete removal would make any sense for me!' *Parsifal* in the Rockies, perhaps, and not in the consecrated temple on the hill? The plan came to nothing.

But preparations for the *Parsifal* premiere – certainly not 1880, but now possibly 1882 – preoccupied him more and more; the Russian painter Paul von Joukovsky, a friend of Henry James, presented himself to Wagner and became one of his circle, as did Engelbert Humperdinck. In the spring of 1880 Wagner enacted the Grail scene with his daughters, Humperdinck and the composer Martin Plüddemann; in Naples, on a journey to Amalfi, he visited Ravello and, after visiting the park in the Palazzo Ruffolo he wrote in the guestbook that 'Klingsor's magic garden has been found!' In Siena he visited the cathedral and knew at once that this must be the model for the setting of the temple at Monsalvat. It was his wish, his command rather, that *Parsifal* be performed only at Bayreuth on the stage devoted to it (Mr Jenkins had, apparently, been forgotten); the King graciously agreed and promised the assistance of the orchestra and chorus of the Munich Court Theatre. Wagner's last meeting with Ludwig was on 12 November 1880 in Munich, when Wagner conducted, for Ludwig alone, the prelude to *Parsifal*. At Ludwig's request the prelude to *Lohengrin* was also performed, conducted by Hermann Levi, son of the chief rabbi in Giessen. It is significant that Wagner should, despite his comments on the Jews in 'Das Judentum in der Musik' (republished under his own name in 1869), insist that Levi should conduct *Parsifal* (Levi's fear that he would have to undergo baptism was initially entertained by Wagner, but subsequently forgotten). Wagner also refused to sign Bernhard Förster-Nietzsche's *Massenpetition gegen das Überhandnehmen des Judentums* (Mass Petition against the Rampancy of Judaism), correctly regarding Förster, Nietzsche's brother-in-law, as a vulgar rabble-rouser. On another occasion, on 21 June 1881, Wagner received an anonymous letter claiming that Levi had had an affair with Cosima (he had been living in Wahnfried at this time). He confronted Levi, who immediately left, whereupon Wagner wrote a passionate letter demanding his return and insisting that Levi 'was *my* Parsifal conductor!'

The incident was rapidly forgotten; in the winter the Wagners left for Palermo, where Wagner finished the orchestration of *Parsifal*'s last act. He sat for Pierre-Auguste Renoir, who drew a portrait sketch of the composer which would later be finished as a painting: this has been described, somehow extravagantly, as showing

> the face decomposed and drained of colour, the eyes rheumy and lips pursed in sickly connoisseurship of sensation; the head is surrounded by an impressionistic blizzard of streaks and daubs, threatening a dissolution of form . . . It is not Wotan's head but Alberich's, feverish, obsessive and expiring.[10]

(Wagner himself would later, on seeing the portrait, prefer to liken himself to an embryo of an angel, or else a swallowed oyster). In Bayreuth, meanwhile, the so-called 'Königsloge' or 'Royal Wing' neared completion, a decorative projection designed to provide King Ludwig with a worthy room where he could rest during the intervals away from the gawping crowds (he already had his own entrance and separate box). The effort and the expense were all in vain, for he never used it, much to Wagner's chagrin.

Rehearsals began in early July under Hermann Levi. Later that month Liszt arrived, as did Anton Bruckner, who knelt before Wagner, whom he deified. The dress rehearsals began on 24 July and the premiere took place two days later. There were fifteen further performances attended by Liszt, Bruckner, Delibes, Saint-Saëns, Nietzsche's sister Elisabeth and Lou Salomé, also Gustav Mahler, who would write to his friend Friedrich Löhr that he had been speechless after leaving the Festspielhaus, knowing that he had received the greatest, the most painful of experiences, something that he would carry with him inviolate for the rest of his life.[11] It was indeed a triumph for Wagner, but a severe heart attack (he had already had minor ones in Palermo), was a warning that time was not on his side.

The audience of 1876 had, sitting in a darkened auditorium, experienced the portrayal of a creation myth, one heralded by the 162 bars of E flat major as through the swirling gloom light strikes into the water. In 1882, they would hear a prelude of such haunting strangeness that Nietzsche, although now an apostate, could only wonder when he heard it some four years after Wagner's death, at a concert in Monte Carlo, if, from a purely aesthetic point of view, Wagner had ever done anything better. It was the supreme psychological penetration that Nietzsche praised, the brilliant expression of every nuance of feeling in the sublimity of the music: this 'does Wagner the highest honour'. Has any painter ever depicted so sorrowful a look of love as Wagner has done in the final accents of his prelude? Nietzsche asked. There is something comparable in Dante, but nowhere else.[12]

The Tristan chord, we know, has entered musical history, but this prelude likewise fascinated musicians such as Debussy, for whom it was 'one of the most beautiful edifices in sound ever raised to the glory of music':[13] the quiet opening on wind and strings, the halo-like hierarchic dignity, the effortless blending in A flat, the intensification in the higher, minor third, the 'Dresden Amen', the bolder theme on the brass, then the massive climax. The final section, a long melody played by searing strings, strives for resolution, conclusion, then finally comes to rest. The strangeness of *Parsifal* is established for the very first bars of the music; this music has entered a place, Virginia Woolf would write in her *Impressions of Bayreuth* (1909), not yet visited by sound.[14] The diaphanous score, searing, longing and ambiguous, its diatonic and chromatic realms strangely interwoven and yet irreconcilable, its fusion of spiritual longing and haunting depravity, its battle between the spiritual and the transient, has fascinated and confused in equal measure. More like a pageant than any other of Wagner's works, its liturgical slowness is necessary for the unfolding of sacerdotal mysteries and rites which are obviously derived from Christianity (baptism and communion); a spiritual impasse is overcome and redemption is achieved.

A brief selection of various expositions will be given before the preferred interpretation is suggested. One eccentric view was that *Parsifal* was a late nineteenth-century reworking of Mozart's *The Magic Flute*, where the masculine realm of light (Sarastro and the Brotherhood) is juxtaposed with, and inimical to, the world of female darkness (the Queen of the Night and her ladies); the fact that Klingsor is allied with Kundry and the flower maidens is explained by the fact that he has castrated himself and lost his virility. In both works the quest is for the return of a precious treasure: the spear in *Parsifal* and, in Mozart, the seven-fold circle of the sun. This was present in the first draft of the opera, the libretto of which was based on A. T. Liebeskind's story *Lulu, oder Die Zauberflöte*, but later dropped. (This sundisc had been worn by the Queen of the Night's late husband but bequeathed to Sarastro, much to the fury of the Queen). Both Parsifal and Tamino have to triumph over the intrigues of the female sex (as Siegfried had resisted the blandishment of the Rhine maidens): Parsifal when ensnared by the flower maidens and, more urgently, by Kundry; and Tamino when he must resist the ladies of the Queen of the Night with their black veils and silver spears. And as Kundry is, finally, accepted by the chivalric order for the final revelation of the Grail, so Pamina with Tamino also enters the Temple of Wisdom. The writer of this fantastical comparison, Arthur Drews, hoped also to see *The Magic Flute* performed in Bayreuth: Nike Wagner, the composer's great-granddaughter, suggests something similar.[15] (It is amusing to recall that after Humperdinck, Rubinstein and Plüddemann were leaving the moonlit villa in Naples in May 1880,

Wagner serenaded them with the air of the three boys from *The Magic Flute,* presumably 'Three boys all young, fair, wise and comely/will be with you upon your journey . . .'.)

The theatre as temple, the stage as a place of cultic ritual: this is what *Parsifal* seemed to represent to many spiritualistic souls at the end of the nineteenth century. Redemptive love and the quest for spiritual transfiguration which were found in the work proved irresistible; the editor of *The Meister,* William Ashton Ellis, insisted that the Master's – Wagner's – music and ideas would help liberate mankind from scientific materialism and stimulate the search for those hidden secrets beyond the world of matter. Ashton Ellis was a Theosophist and the cover design of *The Meister* exulted in symbols of the soul, of divine epiphany and spiritual truth (no wonder G. B. Shaw recoiled on seeing it). A certain Alice Leighton Cleather wrote in her *H. P. Blavatsky as I Knew Her* (Calcutta, 1923) of sinister forces within the Theosophical movement in terms of characters from *Parsifal,* with the villain A. P. Sinnett seen as a black magician forcing Annie Besant to do his will. Cleather airily tells us that Wagner had a considerable knowledge of magic and that he gives us in Kundry an exact and terrible illumination of how 'the plastic elemental female principle' can be manipulated to nefarious ends. The terrible danger to sensitive and hysterical women, apparently, of being subjected to this process by an unscrupulous male hypnotizer cannot be exaggerated, and men like Sinnett, it seems, who had recourse to such evil practices in the pursuit of their selfish ends were black magicians of the worst kind and a menace to humanity. The whole may be taken as a drama of the Theosophical society 'who may now be said to be under the domain of Klingsor, and still awaiting the coming of its Parsifal who can shatter the vast fabric of psychic illusion' (the new Parsifal, apparently, was due to appear in 1975). In Germany, likewise, the symbolism of *Parsifal* merged into the mystic, aesthetic, *Jugendstil* world of Fidus and Franz Stassen and in France the visions of Henri Fantin-Latour.

On a more mundane level, purity and otherworldliness were used in various forms of advertisement, such as Liebig's 'Fleischextrakt' (meat extract), which can, supposedly, cure debility as Parsifal's spear does; also 'Gral Kakoa', a most superior brand of cocoa.

> Take the cast list of *Parsifal*: what a crowd! One extreme, repulsive degenerate after another! A magician who castrated himself; a desperate split personality, half femme fatale and half repentant Mary Magdalene, staggering from one cataleptic trance to another; a love-sick high priest waiting for redemption by a chaste youth; this youth himself, a 'pure fool' and also a redeemer, so different from the bright quick lad who woke Brünnhilde and also, in his way, another weird specimen!

Here, Thomas Mann's great essay 'The Sufferings and Greatness of Richard Wagner' pokes fun at Wagner's last music drama for its bizarre characters, who are reminiscent of one of the stranger manifestations of German Romanticism: Achim von Arnim's *Isabella von Ägypten*, with its carriage full of monstrosities including the Golem and a mandrake called Cornelius Nepos. It is the music, however, Mann concludes, its mythologizing and sanctifying powers, which transcend the abnormalities of Romanticism and allow the work to present a highly religious act of consecration to the world.

A fin de siècle concoction of religiosity and sexuality? A mystic expression of Theosophy and Spiritualism? An oblique derivation of *The Magic Flute*? An exploitation of Christianity for theatrical aims, blasphemous to some, an affront to others? Or something more sinister? The hagiography of the late nineteenth and early twentieth century has given way after the horrors of the Holocaust to find anti-Semitism everywhere in Wagner (in *Die Meistersinger*, as we have noted; also, grotesquely, in *Tristan*). Another extravagant claim is that there is an extraordinary link between the monastic homosexuality of *Parsifal*, centred on the leadership of an intuitively inspired youth, and the not dissimilar fellowship of Ernst Röhm's stormtroopers.[16] It is also reported that Hitler, in a moment of euphoria after successfully occupying the Rhineland, declared on hearing the prelude to *Parsifal* that he would built his religion on this work: 'Divine worship in solemn form . . . without pretence of humility. One can serve God only in the garb of the hero.'[17] It should be remembered, however, that *Parsifal* disappeared from the Bayreuth stage after 1939 for the obvious reason that its twin themes – compassion and renunciation – were meaningless and totally unacceptable to National Socialism. Attempts also to interpret Kundry as a Jewess whose tainted blood would threaten the purity of the knights of Monsalvat are also fallacious: she may have been a Jewess in certain of her reincarnations (Herodias for one, a figure who frequently merged with her daughter Salome in nineteenth-century writing) but was also of Nordic extraction, the wandering spirit Gundryggia, the 'weaver of war' (see Cosima's diary entry of 14 March 1877). Kundry (and Wagner preferred this name with its connotations in German of 'the knowing one') represents a type, the type of the wandering Jew Ahasuerus (see chapter Two); *he* was cursed for failing to show pity and allow Christ to rest; *she* was cursed for laughing at Him, and her accursed, Satanic laugh is only expunged in the Good Friday music of *Parsifal*'s third act, where her penitential tears conquer the hideous cachination.

An apparently esoteric work, then, elusive and open to manifold interpretations. But also a summation, and Wagner's most structured work: an ultimate distillation, as we have noticed, of his lifetime's preoccupations containing a wide variety of elements, dramatic, legendary, intellectual, emotional, musical and philosophical, from his earlier works, including the abandoned *Die Sieger* and *Jesus von Nazareth*. We also remember Wagner's indebtedness to Classical Greece and his draft for an opera, *Achilleus* (1849): Parsifal, who heals Amfortas with the same spear that had dealt the wound, relates back to Achilles who healed Telephos in the same way, in accordance with the oracular pronouncement that 'He who deals the wound shall heal it.' (There are also echoes of Hercules and his freeing of Prometheus, who similarly suffered a wound in his side that would not heal.) It is important to emphasise that the work is *not* specifically Christian despite the incorporation of Christian ritual and symbolism. An all-important essay is Wagner's 'Religion und Kunst' (Religion and Art), written in 1880 and added to later. It may be read as a philosophical complement to *Parsifal* and explains that, when religion becomes artificial, it is for art to save its kernel by recognizing the figurative value of the mythical symbols which religion wishes us to believe as literally true and by revealing their deep and hidden truth by an ideal presentation (x, p. 117). The priest, Wagner explains, is only concerned to have religious allegories regarded as factual truths, but this is of no interest to the artist, who presents his work frankly and openly as his own invention. A distinction is drawn between the *literal* use of symbols by the Church and the artist's *free* adaptation of them. Wagner will use Christian situations in *Parsifal*, baptism and communion, as we have said (and interestingly deconstructing the Mass by inverting transubstantiation), but there is no special pleading for Christian belief. Wagner is reported by Cosima (diary, 20 October 1878) to have objected to Wolzogen's having claimed that Wagner meant Parsifal to represent the Saviour by saying that he, Wagner, never thought about the Saviour at all when creating him; he was fascinated, however, by the rich store of symbols that Christianity had accrued through the ages. It was the theatrical aspect of Christianity, especially Catholicism, which he admired, not necessarily its theological niceties. (We remember his reaction to seeing Titian's *Assumption* in Venice; he also, surprisingly perhaps, defended the papal doctrine of Mary's Immaculate Conception.)

And Buddhism? Its tenets may be found here: the legend of
the killing of the swan; the themes of compassion, abnegation
and renunciation which were also present in *Die Sieger*. It is not
impossible that Christof Schlingensief's production of 2004 had
Buddhistic overtones. Wagner continues in this rambling essay to
look at the various religions (Buddhism, Christianity and Judaism),
but considers Schopenhauer the crown of wisdom. The whole
history of mankind demonstrates the blind raging of the Will;
Wagner lists the world's woes (cruelty, vivisection, meat-eating
and rearmament) and is almost prescient here in his description
of warships and naval bombardment, of sinister monsters of steel
piloted and served by silent, dedicated men, figures who have
lost all semblance of reality (x, p. 162). They seem invincible,
but Wagner talks of torpedoes and dynamite which could sink
them. The main strand running through this concoction is a
Schopenhauerian awareness of the senseless brutality of the
world and the need to transcend this through compassion,
Mitleid. And it will be Parsifal who exemplifies this, the pure
fool who learned what compassion meant, who vanquished the
world of Klingsor, cured the afflicted Amfortas, saved Monsalvat
from decay, removed the curse from Kundry and let the Grail
shine forth in new effulgence. He is the redeemer who redeemed
it, and will live on as ruler and king.

The gentle, brotherly kiss which Parsifal bestows on Kundry
in Act Three is the kiss of *agape*, but the kiss she bestows upon
him in Act Two, the epicentre and mystic heart of the whole work,
is very different. The briefest synopsis will attempt to explain.

The realm of the knights of the Grail, Monsalvat, is suffering
much tribulation since its high priest, Amfortas, the son of Titurel
the founder, languishes in sickness. This is from a wound bestowed
by the spear of Longinus, which had pierced Christ's side and
which, like the Grail itself, is the realm's holiest relic. The stricken
Amfortas bathes each day to ameliorate his suffering; help is often

'Fidus' (Hugo Höppener), an 1896 drawing of a scene from the first act of *Parsifal*, Wagner's final opera (premiered in 1882).

provided, but also proves ineffectual, by a haggard, demonic figure, Kundry; Gurnemanz, an elderly knight, remembers a prophecy about a blameless fool who, chosen by God, and 'knowing through compassion', will one day come to bring salvation. A wild swan is killed by an impetuous youth who bursts in upon the scene; he is

ignorant of his name and is chastised by Gurnemanz for his actions
– he has killed in this holy place. The youth suddenly breaks his
bow and throws away the pieces. Gurnemanz asks him a series
of questions which he cannot answer, but suddenly he recalls his
mother, Herzeleide; at this point Kundry tells him that his mother
is dead, whereupon the youth attempts to strangle her, but is
restrained. Amfortas returns from his bath in the lake and moves
towards the temple; the knights, without taking the sacrament (as
Amfortas, afflicted, cannot administer it, his blood being defiled
for having been seduced by a sorceress and having lost the precious
spear and being wounded by it) wither and weaken, just as the gods
in *Das Rheingold* need the golden apples of Freia to sustain them.
A wondrous transformation scene, to a gentle march rhythm of
great dignity and sonorous tolling bells, has Gurnemanz leading
the young boy to the temple where rituals will be enacted. The boy,
bewildered, feels that he is scarcely moving: Gurnemanz explains
that time, here, has become space, cryptic words indeed.[18] Amfortas
is exhorted to uncover the Grail despite his agonies; the knights
enter, singing a hymn of praise to the sacraments, and Titurel's voice
is also heard, instructing his son to act. Amfortas's great cry of pain,
his screaming for mercy from the all-merciful one, is indeed heart-
wrenching, but he uncovers the Grail and acolytes serve bread and
wine. From on high, voices intone the mantra of the Pure Fool, who
knows through pity and whose advent is promised. Amfortas, whose
wound has reopened, is carried from the hall and Gurnemanz turns
to the youth in irritation: has he understood anything? (He has,
perhaps, not noticed the boy clutch his heart at Amfortas's cries.)
He shakes him, questions him; again he puts his hand on his breast,
but Gurnemanz dismisses him rudely and pushes him out into the
world as, again, from on high, a voice intones the mystic phrase of
the Pure Fool made wise by compassion.

Act Two could not be more different, the prevailing diatonicism
of the first act now replaced by a chromaticism of evil, of sickness

and seduction. This is the realm of Klingsor, and we meet him surrounded by necromantic accoutrements. He had once been a knight of the Grail but now seeks its destruction, having castrated himself. He rules over a magic garden full of seductive flower maidens, who obey his orders to ensnare the knights sent to attack him. For he holds the holy spear, having stolen it from Amfortas while the latter was in the arms of Kundry, and wounded him; he now holds sway over Kundry, who must obey his will. It was Wagner's master stroke to have created this tormented, schizo-phrenic figure – the witch-like hag of Act One with her demonic laughter and convulsive fits here a voluptuous woman. Klingsor calls her up before him and demands that the boy succumb to her charms; at first she resists, wishing to defy him, but Klingsor will prevail (he knows, however, that the one who resists her will free her). He gazes at the youth approaching, at the roses of his cheeks, his boyish beauty (does he also feel regret here at his evil?). The castle sinks and the garden is full of flower maidens, excited and agitated, their vocal lines of laughter rising from the musical turmoil. They then bloom, blossom for this boy; mindless plants, they live only to ensnare him, entwining him with their arms and bodies. But, laughing, he resists them and hears a name called – his name, Parsifal. Kundry, in her voluptuous beauty, calls him from her bower to seduce him by speaking of his dead mother, and bestowing upon him his mother's last kiss.

It is surely not coincidental that Wagner was reading Sophocles's *Oedipus rex* during his work on *Parsifal* in 1877, and the Jocasta–Oedipus relationship may well have been in his mind when he approached the pivotal scene of the kiss; in *Oper und Drama*, some 50 years before Freud, he had commented upon the importance of this myth for an understanding of human nature. To assuage Parsifal's grief at his mother's death (and did not Siegfried cry out for his mother on sinking on Brünnhilde's breast?), Kundry presses a long kiss on his lips, leaning over him. (In the film of *Parsifal* directed by Hans-Jürgen Syberberg in 1982 she does bare her left breast, another reminiscence of *Siegfried*.) It is at this moment that a chord is heard which is the most advanced thing, harmonically, in all Wagner, with purity (the perfect fifth) and impurity (the imperfect fifth or augmented fourth) juxtaposing and converging harmonically as the kiss is given.[19] This is audacious in the extreme and resolved only when Parsifal, in a moment of blinding illumination, leaps to his feet, presses both hands against his heart and screams 'Amfortas! *Die Wunde – Die Wunde!*' ('The wound, the wound!') He identifies with Amfortas whom this same woman had seduced, giving him her body in the knowledge that Klingsor would seize the spear and wound him: Parsifal now sees that her kiss, masquerading as maternal love, was nothing more than lust, and his compassion for Amfortas's suffering has clarified everything. Kundry, meanwhile, in ever growing frenzy, mocks his newly found wisdom: if a kiss had given him this, then full intercourse would make him divine. He knows, however, that this would lead to damnation, and to save *her* he must also redeem Amfortas and the Brotherhood and, indeed the world. In her demented ravings Kundry also sees this: 'Do thou save the world if this thine office be', and he replies that he will also bring redemption to *her*. The dialectic of the arguments of this scene, for both listeners and actors, is one of the most difficult to grasp in all musical history: agony, pain, longing and redemptive love are inextricably mixed and pushed to a terrible intensity. Kundry now attempts to argue that when she laughed at Christ his gaze shattered her and cursed her; she has been seeking his gaze for centuries and now sees that she has found it in Parsifal. One hour with him on her breast and she would be saved. Her kiss has made him wise: her full embrace would elevate him to godlike stature. Finally, her last blackmail attempt to persuade Parsifal to 'pity' her by succumbing is rejected in no uncertain terms by the young man.[20] Kundry becomes increasingly hysterical and confuses him with the Saviour; Parsifal nobly withstands her and she, in raving insanity, calls on Klingsor, who appears with the spear; he throws it at Parsifal and it remains hovering over his head. Parsifal seizes it and makes the sign of the Cross, whereupon the whole sick and demonic realm disintegrates.

The main key for Acts One and Three of *Parsifal* is A flat major; Klingsor's realm, with its connotations of injured pride, resentment, jealousy and malevolence, stands utterly alone between these two acts. The music of the Prelude for Act Three that so impressed Virginia Woolf by its strangeness is an expression of disintegration and chromatic wanderings; the Grail motif inexplicably becomes Kundry's motif until the motif of the Pure Fool is heard again.

It is Good Friday and Gurnemanz, a very old man, finds the Kundry of Act One frozen in the undergrowth (she will only utter two words in this act, '*Dienen . . . dienen*' [to serve, to serve]). He is surprised to see a knight in black armour approach, armed with a spear. He tells him to lay down his weapons, whereupon when the knight thrusts his spear into the earth and removes his helmet. Gurnemanz is amazed to see that it is Parsifal, the fool whom he rejected many years before. Parsifal tells of his aimless wanderings (for the demented Kundry of Act Two had cursed the path that he might wander); Gurnemanz, overjoyed that he has returned, also brings sombre news. Titurel has died, deprived of the sustaining bread and wine after his son's agonizing refusal to uncover the Grail (Amfortas will now be tormented by the guilt of parricide, thus intensifying his already intolerable anguish); the knights have sickened, and Monsalvat was on the point of disintegration. Parsifal, blaming himself for having taken so long to find his way back, is on the point of fainting, but Kundry washes his feet and Parsifal asks Gurnemanz to bathe his head. Gurnemanz blesses him and Kundry, taking a phial from her breast, hands it to Gurnemanz for him to anoint Parsifal as king. This is the great climax as the old man pours the oil over his head to an immense,

Odilon Redon, *Parsifal*, 1891, lithograph.

radiant surge in the orchestra, one of Wagner's greatest acclamations of golden joy. As his first task, Parsifal baptizes Kundry and tells her to believe in the Redeemer. Then follows the famous Good Friday music when Parsifal sees the beauty of the natural world and now, perhaps, we take in the full meaning of Gurnemanz's cryptic words:

'As you have endured the sufferings of the Redeemer, so now you must lift the burden from his head.'

It is essential that the crucial significance of what is happening is here understood. Parsifal, 'having now redeemed himself by insight and empathy, symbolizes a Christ *who does not have to die*, but lives'.[21] Wagner, during the loveliness of that Good Friday music, has Parsifal spellbound before the beauties of the natural world and thereby 'reinforces his anti-transcendent redemptive vision by directing our attention to Nature'.[22] This is what Gurnemanz will tell us: 'No more can creation see Him Himself on the cross: it looks up to redeemed mankind' (IV, p. 327); redeemed, that is, through Parsifal and his deepest compassion for all things. And the memory of that searing kiss of Act Two is expunged by a tender, brotherly kiss on Kundry's brow.

There is but one more thing for Parsifal to accomplish. Dressed by Kundry and Gurnemanz, now his servant, Parsifal takes the spear and the three move towards the Temple (or, rather, as in Act One, they scarcely seem to move; it is the scenery that moves past *them*). Again there is deep tolling of bells, and in the Temple itself a funeral Mass greets the dead body of Titurel in his coffin. Morbid introspection borders here on the histrionic: the frenzied knights implore Amfortas to unveil the Grail and give them the bread and wine of communion. In raving madness he rips open his bandages and begs the knights to plunge their swords into his body up to the hilt. But it is Parsifal who steps forward, touches the wound with his spear and heals him; he then uncovers the Grail, and a divine presence shines forth, redeemed from the power of darkness. Voices from on high announce the Redemption of the Redeemer;[23] Kundry sinks to the floor, now at last dead, her gaze fixed on Parsifal; Amfortas and Gurnemanz kneel before him, and a dove descends to music of utmost serenity.

Parsifal is acknowledged to be one of the most original works of art ever created; an afflicted world is redeemed by compassion and wholeness is restored. Art has here salvaged the nucleus of religion and revealed its truth by means of ideal representation. *Parsifal* is not propagating Christian beliefs, but is 'undeniably a document of the nineteenth-century "religion of art".'[24] It consecrates Wagner's stage, thereby bestowing on theatre, on music, on drama above all, the highest accolade. It is one of the supreme utterances of the human spirit: no more can, or should, be demanded.[25]

The *Parsifal* years and the remaining six months of Wager's life are often described as exhibiting a disturbing, even possibly deranged, lurch in his thinking towards an increasingly irrational, racist and mystical *Weltanschauung*, one that was in keeping with the more unwholesome manifestations of his age and which would besmirch the reputation of Bayreuth for many decades. The influence of Count Joseph-Arthur Gobineau's *Essai sur l'inégalité des races humaines* (1853–5) on Wagner has been much debated; Wagner was drawn to this tract in February 1881 and later read it in the original French. (It is of crucial importance to remember, however, that the text for *Parsifal* was complete in all essentials before Wagner knew of Gobineau's racist ideas and there is no evidence that the Count's distasteful influence can be seen in that work.) Wagner met Gobineau in Italy and invited him to Bayreuth, where he arrived on 11 May 1871 and stayed in Wahnfried for nearly four weeks. There was a good deal of discussion but also much disagreement, and the Wagners were glad to see him go at last. What the visit did produce was Wagner's last supplement to 'Religion und Kunst', entitled 'Heldentum und Christentum' (Heroism and Christianity); it appeared in the *Bayreuther Blätter* and is best understood as a tortuous reply to Gobineau, whose pessimism Wagner could not accept. One thing is certain, he announced to Cosima on 17 December 1881 that the races (that is, Gobineau's differentiation between the base and the superior) had had their day, and the only thing which could save mankind from degeneration was the blood of Christ. A startling statement indeed, and one not easy to grasp.

For Gobineau the white races represented Aryan nobility (with the Jews as sub-Aryans), the yellow represented the *petite bourgeoisie* and the blacks the slave class; through miscegenation with the lower breeds the white races were doomed. In his darker moments Wagner conceded that Gobineau might be correct in seeing decline everywhere but could not forgive his neglecting the chance, given by a heroic suffering saviour, to transcend degeneration. He also suggested to Cosima on 16 October 1882, using Gobineau's crude colour scheme of racial segregation, that the blacks, that is, the lowest order, could become white, the highest, by belief in a suffering redeemer: salvation was possible for all, and this Gobineau could not grasp.

'Heldentum und Christentum' argues that the degeneration has been caused not by miscegenation but by gross materialism, self-indulgence and corrupted blood, blood corrupted, it seems, by the substitution of animal flesh for vegetable food. And it is Christ's pure blood, the startled reader (if there still is one), learns, which can resolve and redeem. The Old Testament God, the tribal Jewish Jahweh, has no place in Wagner's scheme of things, and is rejected; there can be no belief that the Second Person of a Holy Trinity should die in order that the First Person should allow man into heaven.[26] It is a *mystical* belief in a suffering hero which we have here, and the belief that no race (*pace* Gobineau) is beyond salvation seems to be a distant echo of 'Das Judenthum in der Musik', in which, we remember, both Jew and Gentile have to transcend the modern world with its vulgar materialism and seek to become reborn.

But the strident anti-Semitism? It has been emphasized that there is none in *Parsifal* not, indeed, in the whole of his musical and dramatic *oeuvre*, despite Mahler's self-lacerating identification with Mime and the attempts by certain commentators to find it in the most unlikely places (Hagen, for instance, a physical degenerate, a man who, although not literally an onanist, betrays symptoms of this pastime and is somehow an anti-Semitic stereotype).[27] Wagner's voice will never be heard in the rabble-rousing diatribes of Nietzsche's brother-in-law Bernhard Förster, nor in the sermons of Court preacher Adolf Stöcker. Cosima's diaries may well have recorded the dyspeptic outbursts of her irritable husband against the three Js – Jews, Junkers and journalists – but we must also bear in mind her own, far more virulent (French-derived?) hatred of the Jews: it was she who would banish Hermann Levi from Bayreuth in 1884, declaring that he was unworthy and morally and artistically incapable of conducting her late husband's masterpiece, *Parsifal*. She did have the decency to note down both Wagner's statement on 22 November 1878 that, were he writing about the Jews again, he would argue that there was nothing to be said about them except that they had arrived too early among the Germans, who had not been settled enough to absorb them, and his comment on 27 June 1882 to Hermann Levi that Halévy's *La Juive* was a work of great beauty, the finest expression of Jewishness. Wagner's Jewish admirers – Hermann Levi, Joseph Rubinstein, Karl Tausig, Angelo Neumann and Heinrich Porges, among others – were attracted to him by his genius, his superabundant energy, his immensely powerful personality and his idealism; Rubinstein would take his own life in Lucerne shortly after Wagner's death, unable, apparently, to accommodate himself to a world without the Master. Hermann Levi's enthusiastic letter to his father painted Wagner as '*der beste und edelste Mensch*' (the best and most noble of men), even explaining that 'Das Judenthum in der Musik' sprang from the highest motives and was far removed from 'the anti-Semitic calumnies of a Junker or some Protestant toady'.[28] Wagner's world-conquering genius is reflected above all in the music-dramatic masterpieces, also in many of his earlier essays, tracts and plans; the would-be philosopher of his later years frequently lost his way in tangled obscurity. It was finally his misfortune that 'the industrious dwarfs of Bayreuth'[29] selectively mined in the recesses of his last jumbled musings to forge a spiritual sword for Hitler to brandish: Wagner did not create this sinister Nothung. Wagner was too ambitious, too imperious in his artistic creativity to feel the need to incorporate rancorous extraneous material. There is consequently no need, then, to have to listen to him under the proviso that it be only 'uncomfortably'.[30]

The end was not long in coming. The heart attacks became ever more frequent and the Wagners, with Joukovsky, moved in September to occupy the second floor of the Palazzo Vendramin on the Grand Canal. Wagner completed his essay 'Das Bühnen-weihfestspiel in Bayreuth', in which he regretted the problems caused by the transformation scenes; his mood was sombre and he wrote mournfully of the state of the world, its deception, legalized violence and robbery. He gazed he wrote, on nothing but death. Hermann Levi visited him and wrote to his father that he, Levi, was 'intoxicated by joy' on seeing Wagner again. Liszt arrived and composed the piano piece 'La lugubre gondola'; discussion with Wagner turned to the possibility of Wagner's writing symphonies in one movement. Wagner also announced that he intended to rework *Tannhäuser*, that most recalcitrant of his children. He was restless, irritable and prone again to heart attacks. He read an account of Buddha by the Indian scholar Hermann Oldenburg and thought again of *Die Sieger*. On Christmas Eve he celebrated Cosima's 46th birthday by conducting his C major symphony, written some fifty years earlier, in the Teatro La Fenice; in the New Year he was again brooding on *Tannhäuser*, telling Cosima that he owed a debt to the world. Despite reservations about his health he insisted on witnessing the Carnival in Venice with his daughters, Joukovsky and Levi until late into the night; on the following day, 11 February, he set to work on his last, unfinished essay, 'Über das Weibliche im Menschlichen'

Plaque on the Palazzo Vendramin, Venice.

(On the Female Principle in Humanity), which seems to be a tetchy repetition of his jeremiad on the decline of humanity and on human depravity. But monogamy and wedlock amongst the noble races, we read, have elevated man above the beasts. Conventional marriage, however, based on property and possessions has betrayed the specifically human element in marriage based on love between two individuals (x, p. 172); it is touching indeed that an old man was to turn again to those earlier, revolutionary ideas of Bakunin, Röckel and Proudhon, and we recall the plight of Sieglinde and his other heroines. And monogamy, we read, gave way to polygamy as oriental worlds were conquered; there was, however, even in the harems the possibility that an ideal individualistic love could emerge.

On 12 February, Levi, strangely agitated, took his leave; Joukovsky, however, stayed. That evening Wagner read aloud Friedrich de la Motte Fouqué's story *Undine*, that jewel of German Romanticism where water, sensuality and death are hauntingly combined; Joukovsky sketched him. Later, in the night, Cosima

Sketch of Wagner by Paul von Joukowsky, 12 February 1883.

wrote in her diaries, she heard him talking to himself and entered his bedroom where he embraced her, went to the piano and played the lament of the Rhinemaidens from *Das Rheingold*: 'Goodness and truth dwell in the waters; false and base all that which dwells above!' In bed he murmured that he had been faithful to them, these lowly creatures of the depths, these yearning ones.

And his unfinished essay? On 13 February Wagner forewent lunch and worked at it in his study. Woman must be respected and loved for herself. Even the wisest law-giver, even Buddha, could not believe in accepting women as an equal but – and here Wagner hints obliquely at *Die Sieger* (that tantalizing draft for an opera which never left him) – he tells us of a legend which relates how the Buddha *did* admit a woman into his community: Savitri, we remember, will join Ananda as a sister. Passion? Renunciation? Nonetheless, Wagner writes – and these will be his last words – 'the process of emancipation could only progress through ecstatic convulsion: love, tragedy.' (x, p. 174) A massive heart attack seized him and, at approximately three o'clock, he died in Cosima's arms.[31]

'And on the same day a respectfully stunned world received the news of his death.'[32] Thomas Mann's account of the reaction of the world to a fictional death in Venice seems appropriate, as does the response, in D'Annunzio's *Il fuoco* (The Flame of Life) of an overwrought aesthete to the news of Wagner's demise: '*Riccardo Wagner è morte! Il mondo parve diminuito di valore.*'[33] Generous indeed was Verdi's reply to the news. He had once confessed to an interviewer that he stood 'in wonder and terror' before *Tristan*;[34] now, saddened, he wrote to his friend and publisher Guilio Ricordi that a great personality had vanished from the scene, a personality who would leave a powerful mark upon history (he later corrected this to 'most powerful'). The news of Wagner's death came as a crushing blow to Bruckner, who received the telegram from Venice as he was composing his Seventh Symphony, although premonitions of Wagner's mortality had haunted him for days. The great adagio of this symphony uses four Wagner tubas and is reminiscent of Bruckner's *Te deum*; the music of mourning Bruckner composed in D major, however, a key which he felt was more appropriate and expressive. Hans von Bülow felt that his spirit had departed with this 'spirit of fire' (*Feuergeist*). And Mahler? It seemed to him that the brightest star, the guiding light of German music had been extinguished; like Hermann Levi, another Jew, Mahler admired Wagner as a great man as well as a great musician, indeed, as his 'spiritual father'. He had been overwhelmed by *Parsifal* in 1883, claiming that he had undergone the most soul-wrenching experience of his life.[35] Hugo Wolf likewise described *Parsifal* as 'the most beautiful and sublime work in the history of art'.[36] Tchaikovsky, who had made a prophetic statement that something had happened in Bayreuth which 'our children and grandchildren will remember',[37] led Eduard Grieg to announce that he had experienced (in 1876) the greatest music drama of the century and that he fully endorsed Liszt's comment that Wagner's work rose above the epoch's art like Mont Blanc over the Alps.[38]

Are these reactions exalted, effusive, irrational almost? But the least fervent listener would also have to admit that Wagner left behind works of incomparable grandeur dealing with power and love, betrayal and ultimate redemption in music of unparalleled expressiveness; that he bestowed upon further composers as has been noted (Bruckner, Mahler, Richard Strauss, Schoenberg and Alban Berg, for example) a magnificent and flexible instrument of orchestral richness; that his insistence on myth and legend inspired others to create their own worlds, often Celtic, which portray haunting mysteries (in Britain it will be Rutland Boughton who comes to mind with *The Immortal Hour* to be performed at full moon in a forest, or Joseph Holbrooke and his trilogy *The Cauldron of Annwyn*, a fusion, somehow, of *Tristan* and the *Ring*).[39] There are also, finally, the theoretical writings, an immensely fecund source of fascinating insight into theatrical and operatic stagecraft, society and its ills, the need for art to be taken seriously, on love, religion and the role of women. Some of the essays are tendentious; others, especially those written at the end of his life, are tortuous and confused. He is, above all, of supreme importance in demonstrating that it *is* possible for an artistic vision to succeed despite impossible odds. *Sub specie Wagneri* the world will become a more wondrous place, also unsettling, for vistas are opened which challenge and enthral. Yet the immensities of Wagner's vast edifices of sound lift us above the commonplace to archetypal verities and visions: they are life enhancing and speak to the emotions with a unique and exhilarating intensity.

A certain Frau Ottenburg took to her bed on the news of Wagner's death in Willa Cather's *The Song of the Lark*, presumably never to rise again; may the bicentenary of his birth on 22 May 2013 be more of a call to the opera houses and concert halls of the world for performances of his complete canon in exemplary productions.

Conclusion

'Kinder, schafft Neues!'
Children, create something new!

Our introduction told of the re-opening of Bayreuth on 29 July 1951 with a gala performance of Beethoven's 'Choral' Symphony with the Bayreuth Festival orchestra and chorus under Wilhelm Furtwängler; Schiller's 'Ode to Joy' proclaimed that all men were brothers and that a vision of universal harmony had triumphed. Leaflets had been distributed requesting that politics be forgotten, for *'Hier gilt's der Kunst'* (Here art prevails), a quotation from the second act of *Die Meistersinger von Nürnberg.* On the following day Wieland Wager's production of *Parsifal* was performed and shocked many (including the conductor, Hans von Knapperts-busch) by its stark emptiness, without temple, forest, swan or dove: this was indeed *'Entrümpelung'*, a clearing out of dusty encumbrances from the past, the vast stage reduced to a flat round disc upon which isolated figures expressed their *Angst*, their hopes, their fears; there was also a giant cyclorama upon which light was projected. Financial strictures, of course, played a considerable part in this reduction to essentials, but Wieland Wagner demanded that the insistence of the ultra-conservative Wagnerians that only scenery on which Wagner himself had gazed be used, be itself consigned to history. *Die Meistersinger* (with Herbert von Karajan as conductor and Elisabeth Schwarzkopf

A memorial bust of Wagner at Beyreuth.

as Eva) was more traditional, a concession on Wieland's part, but later productions were less reverential, without pomp, pageantry or indeed Festival meadow, which aroused the fury of many. His first *Ring* production was as stark as *Parsifal*; the almost empty stage and skilful use of lighting emphasized the timeless, symbolic meaning of the tetralogy unimpeded by moth-eaten costumes. It was a crime against Wagner, Wieland correctly insisted, to equate his mythic work with the notorious mediocrity of the impotent pseudo-naturalism of nineteenth-century German painting: dogmas and traditional conventions that have no place in the theatre should be expunged, not slavishly followed. 'There is only a present', he explained, 'only a here and now'.[1] Wagner should not be classified as a historical monument; Wieland attacked Hans Pfitzner's demand for a 'German law for the protection of works of art from wilful distortion' and convincingly concluded that those who objected that Wagner's art had been 'betrayed' had not seen that the capacity for being 'betrayed' was perhaps the merit of a great work of art.

In his demolition of tired, stale, lazy conservatism Wieland Wagner spoke of his admiration for Adolphe Appia (1826–1862), the Swiss theatre designer and theorist whose inspired views on stagecraft had, regrettably, not been fully appreciated until the 1950s although tentative beginnings had been made by Emil Praetorius who had known, as had Appia, that the most important tool for any producer was the lighting. Appia had been a fervent Wagnerian from an early age; he had seen Wagner's own production of *Parsifal* in 1882 and also Cosima's staging of *Tristan und Isolde* in 1886 and *Die Meistersinger* two years later. He became utterly obsessed by Wagner's genius but deplored the manner in which this genius was 'totally obscured by the gross burden of contemporary stage practice'.[2] His friendship with Houston Stewart Chamberlain enabled him to get access to the Festspielhaus, not only backstage and at rehearsals but performances as well. Wagner was right to have chafed at the blatant inadequacies of the scenery used in the *Ring* in 1876, but Appia sensed that even he had not realized that any attempt to give his music a completely realistic materialization on the stage was impossible; the interior drama, of overwhelming importance to an understanding of the work, was frequently lost. Appia was adamant that this inner drama could be expressed more fully by light, shadow and colour, also by abstract forms on the stage (he would, had he known, have found it utterly grotesque that the *Ring*, presented some 41 times between 1896 and 1931, used much of the same scenery and was in basically the same style as that first demanded by Cosima). Radically new solutions were needed to express the inner meanings of Wagner's music, but when Appia was finally granted a personal interview with this lady he was coldly rebuffed by her acid statement 'All this has no meaning at all!'[3] And this would be bitterly resented by her grandson, who would admit that Cosima's excommunication of Appia and anathematization of his *Die Musik und die Inscenierung* (Music and the Art of Theatre)

Henri Fantin-Latour, *Immortalité*, 1886, lithograph.

had, for decades, reduced Bayreuth to being a repository of long-dead artistic tendencies and turned its originally revolutionary purpose into its opposite.

Light, then, and abstraction, and strikingly original ideas: it made no sense whatsoever to ask what Beethoven would have made of Toscanini's interpretation of his Ninth Symphony or how Goethe would have reacted to Gustaf Gründgens's production of *Faust* in Hamburg. Wieland's *Tannhäuser* of 1954 set Act Two as a chessboard where the White Queen (Elisabeth) steps from her place to save the Black Knight (Tannhäuser). His production of *Der fliegende Holländer* of 1959 shocked many by the deliberate omission of the Redemption motif (it also shocked his mother, Winifred, who had been excluded from any involvement with Bayreuth because of her admiration for Hitler, by the portrayal of the Norwegian girls in the second act with pendulous breasts hanging almost to their thighs: they were 'udders', not breasts, according to Winifred.)[4] Wieland was also becoming more and more aware of the innovations of Felsenstein and the work of Brecht in East Berlin, and his *Ring* of 1965 with Valhalla as Wall Street and Wotan as an antediluvian Adolf Hitler preparing a more or less heroic funeral for himself showed the direction that Wieland's thinking was taking.

After his untimely death in 1966 his brother Wolfgang, not artistically talented but a shrewd administrator, took charge. To his credit, he kept the ultra-conservatives at bay and demanded that Bayreuth be a 'workshop', trying out new ideas and not flinching from experimentation. In 1972 Götz Friedrich, an East German director very much influenced by Brecht's *Verfremdungseffekt*, was invited. He insisted that there be no self-identification on the part of the actors with the roles they were playing: an ironic stance was encouraged. His *Tannhäuser* caused a storm of controversy by its portrayal of the Wartburg as a ruthlessly vindictive society but above all for the final chorus with the pilgrims, in workmen's clothes, clenching their fists in what looked like a Marxist salute. It seemed to many that Bayreuth had sold out to dangerous left-wing views emanating from the Eastern bloc (and, after all, Bayreuth was only approximately 120 miles from the Czech border). Friedrich's *Ring* also contained an inebriate Fricka and gods who were undeniably degenerate; only the giants – that is, the workers – had a certain dignity. A second *Ring* contained the notorious tunnel which led, apparently, into an unknown future.

The uproar of 1972 was, however, as nothing compared with what happened four years later when Wolfgang Wagner invited two Frenchmen, the young Patrice Chéreau and the famous Pierre Boulez, to produce and conduct the centenary *Ring*, a cultural event of outstanding importance. Boulez, obviously, was a man of experience and distinction; Chéreau, however, had only produced Offenbach's *The Tales of Hoffmann*. But this production proved to be one of the most remarkable and inspiring in recent theatrical history. The Rhine with its hydroelectric dam, the three (dark-haired) Rhinemaidens as trollops, the steam hammer and pit wheel, the Hagen (Karl Ridderbusch) who organized the vassals as though it were a political gathering – this made a tremendous impact. It was felt by many to be a gross imposition: a French *Ring*, a Marxist *Ring*, anathema to the old guard, intolerable, as was the woodbird in a cage and the pantomime dragon pushed about by stagehands. The younger members among the audience were delighted, however, by the humour and the tenderness in the portrayal of love. It was a political allegory of which George Bernard Shaw would have approved, having anticipated it in his *The Perfect Wagnerite*, and is now accepted as a masterpiece of staging, emulated throughout the world.

The way is now clearly signposted by this act of deconstruction: *Regietheater*, or 'Director's theatre', triumphed over Bayreuth, and Marxist ideas proliferated. The East German director Harry Kupfer interpreted Senta's dream in his production of *Der fliegende Holländer* in 1978 as being symptomatic of a somnambulist hysteric whose neuroses were somehow conditioned by society; his *Ring* of 1988 was predictably another criticism of Western society which, in its greed, invariably leads to Armageddon while a bored bourgeoisie watches the end of the world on television.

Brecht's Theater am Schiffbauerdamm seemed to have replaced the Festspielhaus, but there was mounting criticism not only from the *Altwagnerianer* (old Wagnerians); people who had waited ten years for tickets for which they had paid considerable sums of money were hardly likely to be uplifted by banners telling them that they were all Nazis and that Karl Marx was right; to set stormtroopers trampling across the stage in *Parsifal* would not have encouraged them to come again. Wolfgang Wagner seemed to relent in 1983 and allowed Sir Peter Hall to stage his 'romantic', old-fashioned *Ring* (it was, in fact, Sir George Solti, whom Wolfgang had generously invited to Bayreuth to fulfil a lifelong dream of conducting there, who had demanded a 'traditional' *Ring*). The totally naked Rhinemaidens disporting themselves happily in their cool waters while the audience sweltered in the almost tropical heat of a Bayreuth August were obviously delightful to behold, but this 'fairy tale' *Ring* fell between several stools, being semi-naturalistic and lacking a 'Konzept', an intellectual framework. Jean-Pierre Ponnelle's *Tristan und Isolde* of 1986 also refreshingly rejected political allegory and bleak realism: the stage was dominated by an immense tree, symbol of life, love and death, which served as part of the ship in Act One, came magically alive in the moonlight of Act Two and was split and withered in Act Three. (The use of light and reflection on water was also highly effective.) The contrast with Heiner Müller's *Tristan und Isolde* of 1992 could not have been greater: the production was bleakly surreal with the garden of love full of rows of threatening breastplates and the ending eschewing eroticism for an almost Beckett-like estrangement. In the year 2000 a new *Ring* by Jürgen Flimm reverted to a demythologized world with fax machines and shredders, a world thoroughly politicized and loveless. The closing tableau, a young boy in white with a spear, seems to be a Parsifal figure implying that if redemption cannot be hoped for in so heartless and brutal a world, then one would do well to find it somewhere else.

One of Wolfgang Wagner's more remarkable suggestions for possible producers for Bayreuth in 2004 was Lars von Trier, the Danish filmmaker notorious for sensational and often shocking works (*The Idiots*, *Antichrist*); he originally agreed to stage the *Ring* but later withdrew. It is believed that Wolfgang's daughter by his second wife, Katharina (born 1978), suggested that Christoph Schlingensief (1960–2010) be approached; he agreed to produce *Parsifal*. Schlingensief, a provocative young film director associated more with youth culture and grotesque portrayals of the Nazi past than with a stage festival play, seemed to many to be a strange choice, given his predeliction for portrayals of orgasm, excrement and vomit, but invited he was. The beginnings in Bayreuth were not auspicious and an acrimonious atmosphere soon prevailed: Wolfgang was horrified at some of the images proposed and altercations between him and Schlingensief increased; Schlingensief suffered a mental collapse; Katharina intervened and Schlingensief sought psychiatric help. The tenor who was to have sung Parsifal, Endrik Wottrich, denounced the sets as an aberration and made various cutting remarks which were criticized as being racist. Schlingensief also complained of Wolfgang Wagner's parsimonious attitude and poured scorn on the technical staff at Bayreuth for being obstreperous. Against all expectations, the curtain did rise on a set never seen before in Bayreuth and, most likely, never to be seen again.

A slowly revolving stage was packed with a heap of disparate objects and people; the setting hinted at an African shanty town or prison camp (the producer is know to have been interested in Africa, having visited Namibia and proposed an 'opera village' in

Burkina Faso). A black woman with pendulous breasts, wearing only a grass skirt, made an appearance, as did a couple suffering from Down's syndrome, whose nuptials would later be celebrated. Everywhere there were projections from the natural world, also of factories and cemeteries in ruins; many religious figures processed across the stage, leaving bloody handprints on Parsifal, who appeared in white robes. In Act Two Klingsor appeared as a 'negroid' figure, master of voodoo; on his defeat he is dispatched by a rocket into outer space. No Monsalvat, then, no magic garden, and Kundry's later metamorphosis into a callipygian African figure hints that redemption, or whatever this word now means, has very little to do with European Christianity. Schlingensief's teeming imagination necessarily produces a syncretic muddle; his desire to embrace as many aspects of humanity as possible, together with the natural world, must needs fail, but there is something very invigorating in the attempt. My experience of the work in 2007 convinced me that the younger members, again, applauded enthusiastically, accepting the videos, the clutter and the confusion more readily than the older generation. And the decaying hares? A vast screen, as big as the stage itself, gave us the putrefaction and dissolution of this creature in unremitting detail. The hare of Dürer and Joseph Beuys, the hare as a token of fertility, of the lunar goddess Oestra (Easter)? But Hindus and Buddhists also have the hare in their lunar mythologies, as do the Chinese. In his confused way Schlingensief may be telling us that life may emerge from putrefaction and that death need not necessarily triumph. The whole experience which he sought to convey is perhaps akin to a 'near death' experience when the whole of life passes before a dying man. Is this the interval between the death of a physical body and a form of rebirth and reincarnation, the 'bardo' of Tibetan Buddhism?[5] Did Schlingensief know of Wagner's interest in Buddhism? Probably not, but at least his *Parsifal* is mercifully free of swastikas and Nazi uniforms, and most memorable was the conducting of Pierre Boulez in its brilliance and sensitivity. It is indeed a pity that no film was made of the production for future study; Schlingensief did, however, have the words '*Die Bilder werden bleiben*' ('The images will remain') inscribed on one of the few remaining flat surfaces on the stage. They most certainly do.

The depressingly sterile production of *Tristan und Isolde* in 2005 by Christoph Marthaler may be safely consigned to oblivion; it seemed to be in thrall to Heiner Müller's belief that most of those who desire to experience this work in Bayreuth do so to experience something in music that could only bring release after death; a successful production would be akin to a successful public funeral.[6] A dsystopia, then, rather than a celebration of ecstatic oblivion. But this was rapidly forgotten as Bayreuth was about to experience dramatic and far-reaching events which controversially brought tensions and old animosities to the surface. The growing frailty of Wolfgang Wagner led to much speculation on the identity of his successor: his niece Nike, Wieland's daughter, spoke openly of her uncle's senescence and for the need to sweep away what she considered to be hidebound and stupefying in the running of the Festival. Nothing was to be regarded as sacrosanct; she even suggested that the repertoire be extended to include not only Wagner's early operas but also works by other composers, Beethoven and Bruckner, for example, which could be included in a winter festival. (She would later be incensed that the Wagner family totally ignored the bicentenary of Liszt's birth.[7]) Wolfgang dismissed this out of hand and did not conceal his preference for his second wife, Gudrun, to take his place, despite Nike Wagner's reputation of being an expert on drama. Another woman, Wolfgang's daughter Eva Wagner-Pasquier by his first wife Ellen Drexel, also entered the fray, being the favourite of Bayreuth's board of directors for her operatic experience gained at Covent Garden, the Metropolitan Opera House New York and the Opéra Bastille. But then, surprisingly, Wolfgang insisted that his second daughter Katharina supplant her mother and be regarded as his favourite. Katharina's lack of experience obviously counted against her, but her father allowed her to produce *Die Meistersinger von Nürnberg* in 2007: this would demonstrate to the world what she would do. And the 29-year-old most definitely did.

St Catherine's Church had certainly been deconsecrated with apprentices progressing with what appeared to be Bratwürste; much interior decorating seemed to be in progress. Walther von Stolzing, a rebellious, cocky young man wearing trainers, appeared out of a grand piano and merrily helped to slap white paint around. The Mastersingers were formally attired, apart from Hans Sachs the cobbler, who was barefoot and smoked endlessly. Sixtus Beckmesser, with his Reclam texts in hand, insisted that the young noble aspirant (who, apparently, had learned from Walther von der Vogelweide how to draw a naked woman) complete a large jigsaw puzzle of Nuremberg; this he does, but unfortunately upside down. Eva and Magdalene were of similar age and dressed identically as pubescent girls; there was much giggling and whispering. From above plaster busts of German cultural icons looked down: Hölderlin, Schadow, Dürer, Beethoven, Schinkel, Kleist, Schiller, Goethe, Bach, Lessing, Knobelsdorf – and Richard Wagner. In the second act it becomes apparent that Beckmesser becomes a more interesting, progressive figure, not one to be mocked; it is Hans Sachs who cannot move with the times, and delights in hammering on an old typewriter during Beckmesser's serenade. The riot, instigated by the youths of the town, bring the plaster figures to life in an obscene cancan; bottles and books rain down. Good-humoured, if somewhat puerile iconoclasm? But Act Three becomes something far more unsettling, and it is obvious that Katharina Wagner has Hans Sachs in her sights. Sachs, now shod and neatly dressed, commands neither respect nor admiration; Walther von Stolzing is spruced up and respectable: he gains Eva as his bride and a cheque for 10,000 euros appears from above.

The scene on the Festwiese becomes increasingly surreal; the gods of German culture with their giant heads beat each other up and lose fragments of plaster in the process (Wagner loses parts of his nose). On the stage now appear a conductor, a director and a designer; they are also beaten up, killed, and thrown into a large metal skip along with sundry debris and set on fire by Hans Sachs, now, apparently, the guardian of German culture (one of the figures, the director, was a blonde young woman in black: a self-referential joke on Katharina's part: those iconoclasts who dare to step out of line and debunk 'holy German art' are thus punished). Meanwhile Beckmesser creates a naked man out of a heap of soil: he, the outsider, is the truly creative one. But he is dismissed by the onstage audience who divest themselves of their holiday clothes and appear in formal dress – identical, that is, to the audience sitting watching in the Festspielhaus. Now Sachs takes centre stage; lit from behind he casts a huge, menacing shadow across the whole scene in his praise of German art, and two monstrous figures, Goethe and Schiller, Breker-like in their gigantic bulk, rear up sporting rubber dildoes. The German spirit, then, for Katharina Wagner, which is extolled by Sachs is nothing but coarseness and brutality, minatory and blustering: Nuremberg's *Festwiese* becomes Nuremberg's *Reichsparteitagsgelände*. This young woman, smiling radiantly despite the thunderous booing, tried and succeeded in confining her father's very traditional produc-tion of *Die Meistersinger* to the rubbish bin and staked her claim to be taken seriously as an innovative, daring force to be reckoned with. (She had already seen to it that Bayreuth became online with a live webstream transmission of *Tannhäuser*, running a big screen relay of the work and also organizing a 'Wagner for children' scheme including a 'Mini-Ring' which reduces fourteen hours to two.) A few months later, the announcement was made that she and her half-sister Eva would take joint control over the Bayreuth Festival.

An invitation had been sent by Wolfgang Wagner to Hans Neuenfels to produce *Lohengrin* at Bayreuth in 2009; Neuenfels had been a veteran of the demonstrations in 1968 and had been responsible among other things for the notorious production of *Idomeneo* in Berlin in 2003 in which the severed heads of Poseidon, Christ, Mohamed and Buddha had caused an outcry. Neuenfels's vision is certainly another dystopia, ironic, perhaps, rather than confrontational, and even betraying at times something of E.T.A. Hoffmann's *Nussknacker und Mäusekönig* with its seven-headed mouse king. The nobles and commoners of Brabant are portrayed as rats in a modern-day laboratory, the result, possibly, of a clinical experiment that has gone badly wrong; the chorus is composed of rats with snouts, flashing eyes, enormous feet and trembling front paws. These rat costumes may be removed (during the Bridal procession dresses are worn but tails can still be seen trailing across the floor). We are led to believe that their herd-like belief in a better life is fallacious, just as Lohengrin's quest for unconditional love is bound to fail. Elsa is attacked by the rats and pierced with arrows; these, presumably, are the false accusations levelled at her which Lohengrin removes, giving her great pain. She is a figure who cannot compare with Ortrud whose sexuality is quite blatant and who also seeks to seduce *her*. It seems that Lohengrin is the sole survivor of this research laboratory; Telramund is finally reduced to the status of a rat. The future? Gottfried? The finale consists of an adult sized half-foetus slithering from an egg and cutting up its umbilical chord, which it throws out into the world. True humanity, for Neuenfels, is apparently totally impossible; there is no hope, no faith, no love. Again, there was much thunderous booing at the first night, but Katharina Wagner and Eva Wagner-Pasquier stood side by side with Neuenfels braving the uproar, and Angela Merkel spoke enthusiastically of the production later. In 2011 another storm of booing greeted the *Tannhäuser* of Sebastian Baumgarten with its Venusberg as a cage of ape men and tadpoles, its processing plants and drunken shepherd; the song contest had scantily clad girls, a pregnant Venus and a self-harming Elisabeth with Tannhäuser sending cascades of water from above. Elisabeth is finally taken to a vast *Biogas* cylinder and imprisoned. And what, one wonders, will the *Ring* cycle of 2013 bring? Wim Wenders, the renowned film director, had been chosen to produce it but has announced his withdrawal from the project. His successor is Frank Castorf, another controversial director who has been working since the 1990s in the Volksbühne am Rosa-Luxemburg-Platz in Berlin.

The 'children' have indeed, over the last 60 years, created something new, some of it thought-provoking, little of it beautiful, much of it banal, reductive and trite. This book will now end with what the author believes has gone wrong; a more difficult task is to suggest what might be done to redress it.

Wagner's theatre was one of illusion: the two proscenium arches at Bayreuth signify this, as does the sunken orchestra. There is to be a distance between those sitting in the amphitheatre and the action on the stage, thereby enhancing, not reducing, the latter's impact. The inspiration for this, as has been emphasized, was Wagner's interaction with Greek classical theatre, with Aeschylus (in Droysen's translation) and above all the *Oresteia* and *Prometheus Bound* (Hugh Lloyd Jones has described the striking similarities between this latter work and the *Ring*). His theoretical writings also bear this out, and the Swiss writer Gottfried Keller realized, after receiving the privately printed copy of *Die Nibelungen*, that 'a powerful, typically German poetry may be found here, but one ennobled by a sense of antique tragedy.'[8] Myth, then, is paramount, for myth is 'the beginning and the end of history'; when a producer deliberately omits this and foists his or her own interpretation on an audience he may gain a cheap *succes de scandale* but utterly fails to do justice to a work like the *Ring*.[9] When the grandeur

Emil Orlik, *Richard Wagner*, 1898, etching.

and majesty of the music, its oceanic unboundedness, its relentless power of expressiveness and overwhelming force, its portrayal of ecstatic love or cataclysmic disaster – when this music is linked visually to a car park, a brothel or a stock exchange, then profound difficulties arise which no glib reference to *Verfremdungseffekt* can solve. Whether we like it or not, Wagner's stature is colossal: Bryan Magee has rightly claimed that 'he brought together, at the point of their highest development, the mainstream tradition of Western music, the mainstream of Western theatre and the mainstream tradition of Western philosophy',[10] and fused them into works of art that have been unsurpassed. Such a figure, then, deserves more than trivialization and reductive platitudes.

Part of Wagner's greatness resides in his unique ability to invoke the glories of the natural world, from river bed to mountain top, from forest, woodbird and storm clouds to sunrise and rainbow in the *Ring*; shrieking winds and wild waters in *Der fliegende Holländer*; a miraculous transformation and portrayal of spring-like Thuringian meadows in *Tannhäuser*; and the similar portrayal of meadow and flowers in *Parsifal*. It may also be claimed that in Wagner's music we find the greatest invocation of primeval nature in modern art, and when a producer insists on a grimly urban setting, much is lost. But that is something else that must never be overlooked.

Roger Scruton has written eloquently on Wagner's appropriation of myth as being one of the great intellectual advances of modern times.[11] The myth acquaints us with ourselves and our condition, speaking not of what *was*, but of what *is* eternally. 'For Wagner', Scruton explains, 'the heroic love, enshrined in the love of Siegfried and Brünnhilde, was not refuted, but vindicated by its mythical setting.' There is a fund of religious feeling which endows the Wagnerian music dramas with their 'distinctive spiritual glow'. That there is an exalted nobility in much of Wagner's greatest music cannot be denied: some listeners however may baffled at the terms 'religion' or 'spirit'. But Scruton is surely correct in insisting that the moments of sacrifice and renunciation in Wagner have a sacramental quality to which an audience cannot help but respond. Wagner has told us that art, when religion declines, uses religious symbols and situations to salvage essential truths: the *Ring*, Scruton argues, contains moments of genuine religious awe, and to ignore them cynically does untold harm. Scruton likewise, in his *Death-Devoted Heart: Sex and the Sacred in Wagner's 'Tristan und Isolde'* (2004) insists that Wagner's unique masterpiece 'resacralizes a desacralized world' and that the death of the two lovers is a form of redeeming sacrifice; any production that fails to grasp this fails utterly.

The political vein in Wagner has been fully quarried, and it is surely time to look at the heroic, the exalted and the noble, as befits the music. To return to nineteenth-century models would, however, be preposterous; Wagner, we know, was bitterly disappointed when he saw the stage settings of 1876. The natural world must, however, be displayed; abstraction alone would hardly satisfy. We remember how Wagner, at different times in his life, thought of emigrating to America and, indeed, would have taken *Parsifal* with him, leaving Bayreuth bereft. Goethe himself knew that '*Amerika, du hast es besser*', and it is in Seattle that a *Ring* has been produced which has been hailed as that closest to Wagner's heart, going beyond his wildest aspirations, yet truthful to his intentions.[12] The gifts of the courage to be traditional and inventive at the same time, to see and understand the greatness of Wagner's vision and to communicate the glories of the vision in triumphant orchestral sound, are given to few opera houses nowadays, and Seattle has blazed a trail here. It is up to Bayreuth, on the stage which, after all, Wagner's *Parsifal* consecrated, to deal with his greatest themes – sacrifice, heroism, love – with sympathy and conviction; bearskins and horned helmets may be out, but so should computers, dustbins, swastikas, sex shops and sundry vulgarity. It seems that the Seattle *Ring* of the bicentenary year 2013 will be its last; may a European opera house show that it can do even better.

References

Introduction

1 Deryck Cooke, *I Saw the World End: A Study of Wagner's 'Ring'* (London, 1979), p. 264.

2 Quoted in John Deathridge's introduction to Ulrich Müller and Peter Wapnewski, eds, *The Wagner Handbook* (Cambridge, MA, and London, 1992), p. xi.

3 Michael Black, 'The Literary Background', in *The Wagner Companion*, ed. Peter Burbridge and Richard Sutton (London and Boston, MA, 1979), p. 84.

4 Dieter Borchmeyer, *Richard Wagner. Ahasvers Wandlungen* (Frankfurt am Main, 2002). I shall use the English translation by Daphne Ellis, *Drama and the World of Richard Wagner* (Princeton, NJ, 2003), p. ix.

5 Quoted in Bryan Magee, *Aspects of Wagner* (London, 1968), p. 47; Max Nordau, *Entartung* (Berlin, 1893), p. 344. (An English translation, *Degeneration*, was published by Nebraska University Press in 1993.)

6 Magee, *Aspects of Wagner*, p. 50.

7 Barry Millington, ed., *The Wagner Compendium: A Guide to Wagner's Life and Music* (London, 1992), p. 132.

8 Quoted in Raymond Furness, *Wagner and Literature* (Manchester, 1982), p. 30.

9 Martin Gregor-Dellin, *Richard Wagner. Sein Leben. Sein Werk. Sein Jahrhundert* (Munich, 1983), p. 802.

10 See John Warrack's essay 'The Musical Background', in *The Wagner Companion*, ed. Burbridge and Sutton, pp. 85–112.

11 Jonathan Burton in Millington, *Compendium*, p. 334.

12 Nike Wagner, ed., *Über Wagner. Von Musikern, Dichtern und*

Liebhabern. Eine Anthologie (Stuttgart, 1995), p. 153.

13 Ibid., p. 168.

14 Ibid., p. 227.

15 Erik Levi, *Music in the Third Reich* (London, 1994), p. 192.

16 See Roger Boyes, 'Hitler's Record Collection Turns up in Attic of a Dead Russian Soldier', *The Times*, 7 August 2007, p. 3. Great favourites were apparently Chaliapin singing Boris Godunov and Mozart's Piano Sonata No. 8 in A minor.

1 The Beginnings

1 When quoting from Cosima Wagner's diaries I simply give the date. The edition used will be Martin Gregor-Dellin and Dieter Mack, eds, *Die Tagebücher, 1869–1889*, 2 vols (Munich and Zurich, 1977). There is an abridged English translation by Geoffrey Skelton (London, 1978–80).

2 Ernest Newman, *The Life of Richard Wagner* (Cambridge, 1976), vol. 1, p. 60.

3 Richard Wagner, *My Life*, trans. Andrew Gray and ed. Mary Whittall (Cambridge, 1983), p. 37.

4 Barry Millington, ed., *The Wagner Compendium: A Guide to Wagner's Life and Music* (London, 1992), p. 133.

5 For a useful translation see Robert L. Jacobs and Geoffrey Skelton, ed. and trans., *Wagner Writes from Paris* (London, 1973), pp. 44–83.

6 Mary Burrell, *Richard Wagner: His Life and Work, 1913–1834* (London, 1908), p. 108.

7 For a discussion of this work and further valuable insights into Wagner's juvenilia see Dieter Borchmeyer, trans. Daphne Ellis, *Drama and the World of Richard Wagner* (Princeton, NJ, 2003), pp. 1–5.

8 Wagner, *My Life*, p. 68.

9 Ibid., p. 72.

10 John Warrack, 'The Musical Background', in *The Wagner Companion*, ed. Peter Burbridge and Richard Sutton (London and Boston, MA, 1979), pp. 88.

11 Borchmeyer, *Drama and the World of Richard Wagner*, p. 13.

12 Millington, *Compendium*, p. 274.

13 Wagner, *My Life*, p. 124.

14 John Deathridge, *Wagner's Rienzi* (Oxford, 1977), pp. 18–19.

15 Ibid., p. 42.

2 Paris and Dresden

1 Robert L. Jacobs and Geoffrey Skelton, ed. and trans., *Wagner Writes from Paris* (London, 1973), pp. 84–102.

2 Richard Wagner, *My Life* trans. Andrew Gray and ed. Mary Whittall (Cambridge, 1983), p. 215.

3 In a most useful collection of Wagner's more important letters, translated into English: *Selected Letters of Richard Wagner*, trans. and ed. Stewart Spencer and Barry Millington (London and Melbourne, 1989), p. 83.

4 Wagner, *My Life*, p. 230.

5 John Deathridge, *Wagner's Rienzi* (Oxford, 1977), p. 156. (And not only tinsel: apparently Tichatschek was so carried away by his role that he paid 400 thalers for a suit of armour made of German silver but with the accoutrements of solid genuine silver.)

6 See Frederic Spotts, *Bayreuth: A History of the Wagner Festival* (New Haven, CT, and London, 1994), for a description of the original scores which Hitler was given on his fiftieth birthday, including *Die Feen*, *Das Liebesverbot* and *Rienzi*. Presumably these were all destroyed in the final days of fighting (p. 198), Wieland Wagner having failed to persuade him to place them in safekeeping.

7 August Kubicek, *Adolf Hitler mein Jugendfreund* (Göttingen, 1953), pp. 133–42, trans. E. V. Anderson, *Young Hitler: The Story of Our Friendship* (London, 1994).

8 John Deathridge, 'One or Two Things You Ought to Know about Wagner's *Rienzi*', in *Rienzi*, English National Opera programme (1983).

9 H. F. Garten, *Wagner the Dramatist* (London, 1977), p. 37.

10 Thomas Mann, 'Leiden und Grösse Richard Wagners', in *Gesammelte Schriften und Dichtungen* (Frankfurt am Main, 1990), vol. IX, p. 369. An English version may be found in Thomas Mann, *Pro and Contra Wagner*, trans. Allan Blunden (London, 1985).

11 Michael Tanner, *Wagner* (London, 1996), p. 37.

12 For a full account see Curt von Westernhagen, *Richard Wagners Dresdener Bibliothek, 1842–1849* (Wiesbaden, 1966).

13 *Selected Letters*, p. 95.

14 Furtwängler would later, in 1941, call this scene of transfiguration, and Tannhäuser's great cry 'Almighty One, all praise to Thee! Great are the wonders of Thy grace!', one of the most moving in world literature, exhibiting Wagner's genius as a *Dichter*, or poet, able to envisage and express such ecstasy, in Joachim Kaiser's *Richard Wagner* (Hamburg, 1971), p. 262.

15 *Selected Letters*, p. 258.

16 It may be found curious that, in the last act, Wolfram should apostrophize Venus the evening star. But she is now presumably Venus Urania, goddess of divine, noble love, a role imposed upon her by triumphant Christianity. Wolfram, too, loved Elisabeth in his own fashion and now begs the new Venus to guide her through the dark. But she is not long for this world.

17 *Selected Letters*, p. 257.

18 Quoted in Raymond Furness, *Wagner and Literature* (Manchester, 1982), p. 33.

19 *Selected Letters*, p. 138.

3 Revolution, Exile and Reform

1 H. F. Garten, *Wagner the Dramatist* (London, 1977), p. 60.

2 Jack M. Stein, *Richard Wagner and the Synthesis of the Arts* (Detroit, MI, 1960), p. 3.

3 *Selected Letters of Richard Wagner*, trans. and ed. Stewart Spencer and Barry Millington (London and Melbourne, 1989), p. 129.

4 Ibid., p. 248.

5 Heinrich Mann's novel *Der Untertan* (Man of Straw, 1918) describes the obsequious bully Diederich Hessling exulting in the thundering brass; the 'Heil's and Ha's and high-held of banner' Wagner's opera; his ignorance is also lampooned by Mann when Hessling decides to send a telegram to Wagner, not realizing that he had been dead for over 30 years.

6 Elizabeth Magee, *Richard Wagner and the Nibelungs* (Oxford, 1990), p. 3.

7 Quoted in Jon W. Finson and R. Larry Todd, eds, *Mendelssohn and Schumann: Essays on their Music and its Context* (Durham, NC, 1984), p. 25.

8 Garten, *Wagner the Dramatist*, p. 63.

9 Richard Wagner, trans. Andrew Gray and ed. Mary Whittall, *My Life* (London, 1983), p. 387.

10 Ibid., pp. 342–3.

11 Richard Wagner, trans. R. L. Jacobs, *Three Wagner Essays* (London, 1979), p. viii.

12 Stein, *Richard Wagner and the Synthesis of the Arts*, pp. 161–2.

13 Wagner, *My Life*, p. 436.

14 See, for example, *Sämtliche Briefe*, ed. Gertrud Strobel and Werner Wolf (Leipzig, 1975), vol. III, p. 248f. I am also indebted here to O. G. Bauer's article, 'Der falsche Prophet', in *Wagner und die Juden*, ed. Dieter Borchmeyer, Ami Maayani and Susanne Vill (Stuttgart and Weimar, 2000), pp. 271–95.

15 *Selected Letters*, p. 185.

16 *Sämtlichte Briefe*, III, p. 249.

17 Wagner's almost schizophrenic attitude to Paris may be seen in a letter to King Ludwig (18 July 1867) in which the city is extolled as 'the culminating point; all other cities are simply stages on the way.' It is the heart of modern civilization, and Wagner is grateful to his 'good angel' from having sent him there: *Sämtlichte Briefe*, ed. Margaret Jestremski et al. (Wiesbaden, 2011), vol. XIX.

18 Martin Gregor-Dellin, *Richard Wagner. Sein Leben. Sein Werk. Sein Jahrhundert* (Munich, 1983), p. 299.

19 Tibor Kneif, ed., *Richard Wagner. Die Kunst und die Religion. Das Judentum in der Musik. Was ist deutsch?* (Munich, 1975), pp. 115–16.

20 Bryan Magee, *Aspects of Wagner* (London, 1968), pp. 38–9.

21 Kneif, ed., *Richard Wagner*, pp. 76–7.

22 See Dieter Borchmeyer, trans. Daphne Ellis, *Drama and the World of Richard Wagner* (Princeton, NJ, 2003), p. 99 for an explanation of the word 'Untergang'.

23 See Dieter Borchmeyer's article 'Richard Wagner and Anti-Semitism', *Wagner*, VI/1 (January 1985).

24 *Selected Letters*, p. 216.

25 Ibid.

26 See Klaus Kropfinger, *Oper und Drama* (Stuttgart, 1984), pp. 149–50.

27 For a perceptive discussion of Feuerbach see Bryan Magee, *Wagner and Philosophy* (London, 2000), chapter 4.

28 P. J. Branscombe, 'Wagner as Poet', in Andrew Porter, *Richard Wagner, 'The Ring'* (Chatham, 1976), pp. xxix–xli.

29 Thomas S. Grey, 'A Wagnerian Glossary', in *The Wagner Compendium: A Guide to Wagner's Life and Music*, ed. Barry Millington (London, 1992), p. 235.

4 Exploration and Consolidation

1 Richard Wagner, *My Life*, trans. Andrew Gray and ed. Mary Whittall (Cambridge, 1983), p. 499.

2 Ibid.

3 Barry Millington, ed., *The Wagner Compendium: A Guide to Wagner's Life and Music* (London, 1992), pp. 135.

4 Deryck Cooke, *I Saw the World End: A Study of Wagner's 'Ring'*, (London, 1979), p. 134.

5 Bryan Magee, *Wagner and Philosophy* (London, 2000), p. 111.

6 Ibid., p. 115.

7 See the letter to Röckel, 25/26 January 1854 in *Selected Letters of Richard Wagner*, trans. and ed. Stewart Spencer and Barry Millington (London and Melbourne, 1989), pp. 300–12.

8 Magee, *Wagner and Philosophy*, p. 132.

9 Wagner, *My Life*, p. 510.

10 *Selected Letters*, p. 323. Schopenhauer reported that he had received a letter from a group of admirers in Zurich; a certain Richard Wagner had sent him a libretto, on impressively thick paper and neatly bound, of the *Ring des Nibelungen* which he intended to set to music. It was to be 'The Art-work of the Future'. Schopenhauer, who preferred Rossini, regarded it as a fantastical concoction and did not reply. He also commented that Wagner was a dramatist and should give up trying to be a composer.

11 Rupert Christiansen, 'Kultur-Clash: Richard Wagner in London', *Daily Telegraph*, 22 April 2000.

12 *Selected Letters*, p. 349.

13 Wagner, *My Life*, p. 511.

14 H. F. Garten, *Wagner the Dramatist* (London, 1977), p. 199.

15 See Rudolph Sabor, '"Tristan und Isolde" and its Current Bayreuth Staging', *Wagner*, VIII/2 (April 1987).

16 Magee, *Wagner and Philosophy*, p. 199.

17 Wagner, *My Life*, p. 509.

18 Erich Heller, *The Ironic German: A Study of Thomas Mann* (London, 1958), p. 29.

19 Magee, *Wagner and Philosophy*, p. 175.

20 Robert Gutman, in his *Richard Wagner: The Man, His Mind and His Music* (New York, 1965), p. 117, explains ironically that many of Wagner's characters were disciples of Schopenhauer before their creator grasped the doctrine guiding their steps.

21 Dieter Borchmeyer, trans. Daphne Ellis, *Drama and the World of Richard Wagner* (Princeton, NJ, 2003), p. 156.

22 *Selected Letters*, p. 165.

23 Ibid., p. 432.

24 Friedrich Nietzsche, *Sämtliche Werke: Kritische Studienausgabe*, ed. Giorgio Colli and Mazzino Montinari (Munich, 1980), vol. VIII, p. 191.

25 Jack M. Stein, *Richard Wagner and the Synthesis of the Arts* (Detroit, MI, 1960), p. 131.

26 Whether or not the lovers, in their duet in Act Two, ejaculate orgasm simultaneously seven times is certainly open to dispute, but Virgil Thomson believed so and claimed that it was 'clearly marked in the music' (Millington, *Compendium*, p. 300). The haute couture photographer Erwin Blumenfeld also claimed that he was conceived at midnight on 5 May 1896 in Berlin in a carriage that was taking his parents home after seeing *Tristan und Isolde*.

27 Martin Gregor-Dellin, *Wagner Chronik* (Munich, 1972), p. 86. It would indeed be prurient to speculate on the sexual nature of the relationship between Wagner and Mathilde; William Ashton Ellis, who met Mathilde briefly, insisted that she was 'a placid, sweet Madonna, the perfect emblem of a pearl, not opal, her eyes still dreaming of Nirvana – no! emphatically no! – she could not once have been swayed by carnal passion' (in *Kunstwerk der Zukunft. Richard Wagner und Zürich (1849–1858)*, ed. Laurenz Lütteken [Zürich, 2008], p. 98). We shall meet Ashton Ellis later in chapter Six where we consider his theosophical leanings.

28 Wagner also met Rossini: see Edmond Michotte's entertaining account *Richard Wagner's Visit to Rossini*, trans. Herbert Weinstock (London, 1992), pp. 9–90.

29 Raymond Furness, *Wagner and Literature* (Manchester, 1982), p. 33. Baudelaire's brilliant essay 'Richard Wagner et *Tannhäuser* à Paris' (Paris, 1861) will recapture the thrill, the exhilaration and the full force of the rapturous bacchanal: the 'complete onomatopoeic dictionary of love' is heard here.

30 *Selected Letters*, pp. 486–91.

31 This painting had a remarkable effect on Wagner, who described it to Cosima on 8 December 1880 as representing sublimated desire and the ecstasy of love; two years later, on 22 October 1882, he is reported by Cosima in her diary to have claimed that the woman on the canvas is not the mother of God but Isolde in the apotheosis of love.

32 Wagner, *My Life*, p. 667.

33 *Selected Letters*, p. 572. This 'pink drawers' reference has, understandably, never failed to intrigue: the Kölner Theaterhaus staged Bernd Wessling's *Cosimo und Ricarda* in 2010, a scurrilous portrayal of Wagner's ostensible penchant for female underwear. The composer dreams of Judith Gautier while his wife, in riding breeches and jackboots, acts the part of dominatrix (it is she who wears Wagner's famous beret). The rest may be imagined.

34 Wagner, *My Life*, p. 729. This last sentence was deleted from *My Life* in all editions before 1963.

5 World Fame

1 A death-fixated work? Schnorr had sung the part at the National Theatre, Munich; in 1911 the conductor Felix Mottl collapsed during a performance there and died four days later; in 1968 Joseph Keilberth suffered a fatal heart attack immediately after Isolde's words '*ohn' Erwachen*' ('without awakening') in the love duet in Act Two (Dieter Borchmeyer, trans. Daphne Ellis, *Drama and the World of Richard Wagner* [Princeton, NJ, 2003], p. 158).

2 Two years before, another visitor had arrived unexpectedly to see Wagner (this time in Haus Pellet) using a Wagnerian soubriquet: the

socialist Ferdinand Lassalle, announcing himself as 'Siegfried', shortly before his death in a duel.

3 Friedrich Nietzsche, *Sämtliche Werke: Kritische Studienausgabe*, ed. Giorgio Colli and Mazzino Montinari (Munich, 1980), vol. v, p. 179.

4 Hans Rudolf Vaget, 'Wagner, Anti-Semitism and Mr Rose's Merkwürd'ger Fall!', *The German Quarterly*, lxvi/2 (Spring 1993) provides an excellent riposte to Paul Lawrence Rose's claim that the anti-Semitism in *Die Meistersinger* is undeniably crude.

5 Barry Millington, 'Nuremberg Trial: Is There Anti-Semitism in *Die Meistersinger?*', *Cambridge Opera Journal*, 3 (1991) and also in Millington, ed., *The Wagner Compendium: A Guide to Wagner's Life and Music* (London, 1992), in a discussion of Grimm's story *Der Jude im Dorn* and its relevance to Walther's outburst at the end of Act One of *Die Meistersinger*, p. 304. For Borchmeyer's rebuttal see Borchmeyer, trans. Ellis, *Drama and the World of Richard Wagner*, pp. 202–9. To compare, as Eva does, Wather von Stolzing with Dürer's image of David slaying Goliath, and to remind us that King David and his harp are noble images of the Meister's Guild, hardly indicate rampant anti-Semitism on Wagner's part.

6 In a letter to Erwin Rohde of 9 November 1868: Karl Schlechta, ed., *Friedrich Nietzsche. Werke in drei Bänden* (Munich, 1966), vol. iii, pp. 999–1000. This letter confirms that Wagner was at his best in a small group which he could *dominate*; he could also play the clown and enjoyed imitating the Leipzig dialect.

7 *Selected Letters of Richard Wagner*, trans. and ed. Stewart Spencer and Barry Millington (London and Melbourne, 1989), pp. 757–8.

8 See Thomas S. Gray, 'Eduard Hanslick on Wagner's *Beethoven*', *Wagner*, xv/2 (May 1994), pp. 51–7.

9 In *Das braune Buch*, ed. Joachim Bergfeld (Munich, 1975), p. 215. This has been translated into English by George Bird: *The Diary of Richard Wagner, 1865–1882*, ed. Joachim Bergfeld (London, 1980).

10 *Selected Letters*, p. 824.

11 Ibid.

12 G. B. Shaw, *Major Critical Essays*, in the *Standard Edition of the Works of George Bernard Shaw* (London, 1948), p. 201.

13 See Joachim Herz, 'The Figure and Fate of Wotan in Wagner's "Ring"', *Wagner*, xv/2 (May 1994), p. 95.

14 *Selected Letters*, p. 873.

15 Roger Scruton, 'Pilgrims on the Way to Extinction', *Times Literary Supplement*, 7 March 1997.

16 Thomas Mann, 'To the Editor of Common Sense', in *Wagner und Unsere Zeit. Aufsätze, Betrachtungen, Briefe*, ed. Erika Mann (Frankfurt am Main, 1963), p. 156.

17 Carl Dahlhaus, *Richard Wagner's Music Dramas*, trans. Mary Whittall (Cambridge, 1979), p. 109.

18 *Selected Letters*, p. 859.

19 Wilhelm Blisset, 'The Liturgy of *Parsifal*', *University of Toronto Quarterly*, XLIX/2 (Winter 1979–80), p. 117.

6 Consummation

1 *Selected Letters of Richard Wagner*, trans. and ed. Stewart Spencer and Barry Millington (London and Melbourne, 1989), p. 457.

2 Richard Wagner, *My Life*, trans. Andrew Gray and ed. Mary Whittall (London, 1983), p. 547.

3 *Selected Letters*, pp. 499–501.

4 See Dieter Borchmeyer, ed., *Dichtungen und Schriften* (Frankfurt am Main, 1983), vol. IV, p. 293, for reference to his earlier process.

5 Carl Dahlhaus, *Richard Wagner's Music Dramas*, trans. Mary Whittall (Cambridge, 1979), p. 144.

6 See Rupert Christiansen, 'Kultur-Clash: Richard Wagner in London', *Daily Telegraph*, 22 April 2000.

7 Mary A. Cicora, *'Parsifal' Reception in the 'Bayreuther Blätter'* (New York, 1987), p. 25.

8 Max Nordau, *Entartung* (Berlin, 1893), p. 175.

9 *Selected Letters*, p. 899.

10 Peter Conrad, 'Unmasking the Master', *Times Literary Supplement*, 23 July 1976.

11 Nike Wagner, ed., *Über Wagner. Von Musikern, Dichtern und Liebhabern. Eine Anthologie* (Stuttgart, 1995), p. 180.

12 In a letter to Peter Gast, 21 January 1887: Karl Schlechta, ed., *Friedrich Nietzsche. Werke in drei Bänden* (Munich, 1966), vol. III, p. 1249.

13 In *Debussy on Music*, trans. R. Langham-Smith (New York, 1977),

p. 167. *Parsifal* also haunts Elgar's *The Dream of Gerontius* (but Elgar resists his friend Jaeger's insistence that Elgar emulate Wagner in expressing the soul's glimpse of God in a far more tremendous, dramatic way). Elgar would later leap to the defence of Wagner after the canon of Worcester Cathedral denounced him as a 'sensualist'.

14 In Raymond Furness, *Wagner and Literature* (Manchester, 1982), p. 2.

15 See, for example, her article, 'Kinder Schafft Neues' in the *Frankfurter Allgemeine* (30 May 2000).

16 Robert Gutman, *Richard Wagner: The Man, His Mind and His Music* (New York, 1965), p. 300.

17 Joachim C. Fest, *Hitler* (London, 1974), p. 741.

18 This gnomic utterance is best understood as a result of Wagner's study of Jewish mysticism where he found the concept, in Philo, of God as absolute space which existed prior to time and is in consequence superior to it. See the essay by Wolf-Daniel Hartwich on Wagner and Cabbalism, 'Jüdische Theosophie in Richard Wagners "Parsifal"', in *Wagner und die Juden*, ed. Dieter Borchmeyer, Ami Maayani and Susanne Vill (Stuttgart and Weimar, 2000), pp. 103–22.

19 See the essay by Ian Beresford Gleaves, 'Parsifal – No Enigma', *Wagner News*, no. 147 (September 2001).

20 It should in no way be understood that Wagner is preaching celibacy here; there is no condemnation of sexual activity per se. Parsifal here seeks to free Kundry from her tormented belief in self-salvation through seduction, and in this he will succeed. The Knights may be celibate and fear women, but their reaction is hardly exemplary. And Parsifal, as we know, will become a father.

21 Quoted from Robert Raphael in Michael Tanner, 'The Total Work of Art', in *The Wagner Companion*, ed. Peter Burbridge and Richard Sutton (London and Boston, MA, 1979), p. 215.

22 Ibid., p. 216. I am most indebted to Michael Tanner for his insights here.

23 There has been much wild speculation as to the meaning of these words, some even declaring that it is Wagner who is redeeming Christ (a task which even he would not arrogate to himself). They simply mean that the Grail has been liberated from Amfortas's sick administration and many now shine forth. It is also erroneous to claim that these words were inscribed on Wagner's grave. The grave bears no inscription.

24 Dahlhaus, *Richard Wagner's Music Dramas*, p. 144.

25 See Lucy Beckett's Cambridge Opera handbook *Parsifal* (Cambridge, 1981) for a specifically Christian interpretation of the work.

26 Tanner, *The Wagner Companion*, p. 216.

27 See chapter 5, 'Icons of Degeneration', in Marc A. Weiner's *Richard Wagner and the Anti-Semitic Imagination* (Lincoln, NE, and London, 1995).

28 Martin Gregor-Dellin, *Wagner Chronik* (Munich, 1972), p. 167.

29 See David Large's 'Wagner's Bayreuth Disciples', in David C. Large and William Weber, *Wagnerism in European Culture and Politics* (Ithaca, NY, and London, 1984), p. 133.

30 See Paul Lawrence Rose's letter to the *Times Literary Supplement*, 1 August 2008.

31 There has been a rumour that Wagner's last heart attack was caused by a furious argument between him and his wife over a certain Carrie Pringle, an English girl and one of the flower-maidens, to whom Wagner was attracted. Those wishing to follow this up are referred to Stewart Spencer's demolition 'Er starb, ein Mensch wie alle: Wagner and Carrie Pringle', *Wagner*, xxv/2 (September 2004).

32 Martin Gregor-Dellin, *Richard Wagner. Sein Leben. Sein Werk. Sein Jahrhundert* (Munich, 1983), p. 842.

33 Gabrielle D'Annunzio, *Il fuoco* (Milan, 1977), p. 338.

34 Barry Millington, ed., *The Wagner Compendium: A Guide to Wagner's Life and Music* (London, 1992), p. 382.

35 See Wagner, ed., *Über Wagner*, p. 180.

36 Millington, *The Wagner Compendium*, p. 381.

37 Ibid.

38 Ibid.

39 Holbrooke, to outdo Wagner, demanded a sarrusophone for his gigantic orchestra, a double-reed instrument classified as a woodwind but made of brass; a double-bass sarrusophone is something like a double bassoon. One was finally found for him in France.

Conclusion

1 For an English version of Wieland Wagner's lecture delivered to the Society of the Friends of Bayreuth (25 July 1958) see *Wagner*, xii/3

(September 1991), pp. 137–44.

2 In Richard C. Beacham, *Adolphe Appia, Theatre Artist* (Cambridge, 1987), p. 14.

3 Ibid., p. 41.

4 Brigitte Hamann, *Winifred Wagner und Hitlers Bayreuth* (Munich, 2003), p. 587. (This has been translated and abridged by Alan Bance as *Winifred Wagner: A Life at the Heart of Hitler's Bayreuth* (London, 2005).

5 See *Wagner News*, 172 (February 2006) for an article by Paula and Edward Bortnichak on 'Parsifal: Bayreuth as Bardo'.

6 See the review by Claus Spahn in *Die Zeit* (31/2005).

7 Her cousin Katharina Wagner would, however, feel honoured to act as patroness of the Israel Chamber Orchestra who played, in 2011, a concert entitled 'Lust auf Liszt' in the Stadthalle in Bayreuth. They would also, moreover, play the *Siegfried Idyll*.

8 Raymond Furness, *Wagner and Literature* (Manchester, 1982), p. 73.

9 A brave attempt was made by Alfred Kirchner in his *Ring* of 1994–8 to take the mythological status of Wagner's tetralogy seriously, rejecting the demythologizing tendency which had become de rigueur in Bayreuth and elsewhere. Kirchner sought to reactivate myth, but not placing it in the past: myth was to be encapsulated in its remoteness but also in its closeness to us. But the production failed to reconcile the archetypal with modern gimmicry, resulting in stylistic confusion and often risible stage effects (stylistic Valkyries, for example, swinging vertically and horizontally in individual lifts, and pale green telegraph posts/trees which were hinged to allow their tops to bow in mourning at Siegfried's death).

10 Bryan Magee, *Wagner and Philosophy* (London, 2000), p. 193.

11 Scruton's excellent article 'Descrating Wagner' was reprinted in *Wagner News*, 161 (March 2004), pp. 11–17, and I am much indebted to it.

12 For a description of the Seattle production see the review by Paul Dawson-Bowling, 'Wunder muss ich euch melden', *Wagner News*, 148 (December 2001), pp. 5–8.

Select Bibliography

Adorno, Theodor, *In Search of Wagner*, trans. Rodney Livingstone (London, 1981)

Beckett, Lucy, *Parsifal*, Cambridge Opera Handbook (Cambridge, 1981)

Borchmeyer, Dieter, ed., *Dichtungen und Schriften*, 10 vols (Frankfurt am Main, 1983)

——, ed., *Wege des Mythos in der Moderne* (Munich, 1987)

——, *Richard Wagner: Theory and Theatre*, trans. Stewart Spencer (Oxford, 1991)

——, *Drama and the World of Richard Wagner*, trans. Daphne Ellis (Oxford, 2003)

Burbidge, P., and R. Sutton, eds, *The Wagner Companion* (London and Boston, MA, 1979)

Burrell, Mary, *Richard Wagner: His Life and Work from 1813–1834* (London, 1898)

Carnegy, Patrick, *Wagner and the Art of the Theatre* (London, 2006)

Carr, Jonathan, *The Wagner Clan* (London, 2007)

Cooke, Deryck, *I Saw the World End: A Study of Wagner's 'Ring'* (London, 1979)

Dahlhaus, Carl, *Richard Wagner's Music Dramas*, trans. Mary Whittall (Cambridge, 1979)

Deathridge, John, *Wagner's 'Rienzi': A Reappraisal Based on a Study of the Sketches and Drafts* (Oxford, 1977)

——, and Carl Dahlhaus, *The New Grove Wagner* (London, 1984)

——, Martin Geck and Egon Voss, *Wagner Werk-Verzeichnis* (Mainz, 1986)

Donnington, Robert, *Wagner's 'Ring' and its Symbols: The Music and the Myth* (London, 1963)

Dzamba Sessa, Anne, *Richard Wagner and the English* (Rutherford, NJ, 1979)

Ellis, William Ashton, trans., *Richard Wagner's Prose Works*, 8 vols (London, 1895–9; reprinted New York, 1966, and Lincoln, NE, 1993–5)

English National Opera and the Royal Opera Guides: *Tristan und Isolde* (London, 1981); *Der fliegende Holländer* (London, 1982); *Die Meistersinger* (London, 1985); *Die Walküre* (London, 1983); *Siegfried* (London, 1984); *Götterdämmerung* (London, 1985); *Das Rheingold* (London, 1985); *Tannhäuser* (London, 1988)

Ewans, Michael, *Wagner and Aeschylus: The 'Ring' and the 'Oresteia'* (London, 1982)

Field, Geoffrey G., *Evangelist of Race: The Germanic Vision of Houston Stewart Chamberlain* (New York, 1981)

Gutman, Robert, *Richard Wagner: The Man, his Mind and his Music* (New York, 1968)

Hamann, Brigitte, *Winifred Wagner: A Life at the Heart of Hitler's Bayreuth*, trans. Alan Bance (London, 2005)

Hartford, Robert, *Bayreuth: The Early Years* (London, 1980)

Hollinrake, Roger, *Nietzsche, Wagner and the Philosophy of Pessimism* (London, 1982)

Jacobs, R. L., trans., *Three Wagner Essays* (London, 1979)

Katz, Jacob, *The Darker Side of Genius: Richard Wagner's Anti-Semitism* (London, 1986)

Koehler, Joachim, *Richard Wagner: The Last of the Titans*, trans. Stewart Spencer (London, 2004)

Koppen, Erwin, *Dekadenter Wagnerismus* (Berlin, 1973)

Kubizek, August, *Young Hitler: The Story of Our Friendship*, trans. E. V. Anderson (London, 1954)

Langer, Axel, and Chris Walton, eds, *Minne, Muse und Mäzen. Otto und Mathilde Wesendonck und ihr Zürcher Künstlerzirkel* (Zürich, 2002)

Large, David C., and William Weber, eds, *Wagnerism in European Culture and Politics* (Ithaca, NY, 1985)

Levi, Erik, *Music in the Third Reich* (London, 1994)

Mack, Dietrich, ed., *Cosima Wagner. Das zweite Leben. Briefe und Aufzeichnungen, 1983–1930* (Munich, 1980)

Magee, Bryan, *Aspects of Wagner* (London, 1972; new and enlarged edition Oxford, 1988)

——, *Wagner and Philosophy* (London, 2002)

Magee, Elizabeth, *Richard Wagner and the Nibelungs* (Oxford, 1990)

Mann, Thomas, 'Leiden und Größe Richard Wagners', in *Die Neue Rundschau*, IV/44 (April 1933)

——, *Pro and Contra Wagner*, trans. Allan Blunden and ed. Patrick Carnegy, with an introduction by Erich Heller (London, 1985)

Millington, Barry, *Wagner* (London, 1984)

——, 'Nuremberg Trial: Is there Anti-Semitism in *Die Meistersinger?*', *Cambridge Opera Journal*, III/3 (1991)

——, ed., *The Wagner Compendium: A Guide to Wagner's Life and Music* (London, 1992)

——, and Stewart Spencer, eds, *Wagner in Performance* (London, 1992)

Müller, Ulrich, and Peter Wapnewski, eds, *Richard-Wagner-Handbook* (Stuttgart, 1986), translation ed. John Deathridge (London, 1992)

Newman, Ernest, *The Wagner Operas* (New York, 1949; reprinted 1961, 1977, 1988)

——, *The Life of Richard Wagner*, 4 vols (Cambridge, 1976)

Nietzsche, Friedrich, *The Case of Wagner: Nietzsche contra Wagner*, trans. Anthony M. Ludovici (London, 1910)

——, *The Birth of Tragedy and The Case of Wagner*, trans. Walter Kaufmann (New York, 1967)

——, 'Nietzsche contra Wagner: From the Files of a Psychologist', in *The Portable Nietzsche*, ed. and trans. W. Kaufmann (New York, 1976)

——, *Ecce Homo*, trans. R. J. Hollingdale (Cambridge, 1983)

——, *Untimely Meditations*, trans. R. J. Hollingdale (Cambridge, 1983)

Rose, Paul Lawrence, *Wagner: Race and Revolution* (London, 1992)

Scruton, Roger, *Death-devoted Heart: Sex and the Sacred in Wagner's 'Tristan und Isolde'* (Oxford, 2004)

Shaw, George Bernard, *The Perfect Wagnerite: A Commentary on the Nibelung's Ring* (London, 1898; 4th edn 1923; reprinted 1972)

Spencer, Stewart, and Barry Millington, trans. and ed., *Selected Letters of Richard Wagner* (London, 1989)

Spencer, Stewart, and Barry Millington, *Wagner's Ring of the Nibelung: A Companion* (London, 1995)

——, ed., *Wagner Remembered* (London, 2000)

——, 'The "Romantic" Operas and the Turn to Myth', in *The Cambridge Companion to Wagner*, ed. Thomas S. Grey (Cambridge, 2011)

Spotts, Frederic, *Bayreuth: A History of the Wagner Festival* (London, 1994)

Stein, Jack M., *Richard Wagner and the Synthesis of the Arts* (Detroit, MI, 1960; reprinted 1973)

Sutton, Emma, *Aubrey Beardsley and British Wagnerism in the 1890s* (Oxford, 2002)

Syberberg, Hans Jürgen, *Parsifal: Ein Filmessay* (Munich, 1982)

Tanner, Michael, *Wagner* (London, 1996)

——, *Wagner: A Pocket Guide* (London, 2010)

Taylor, Ronald, trans., *Furtwängler on Music* (Aldershot, 1991)

Treadwell, James, *Interpreting Wagner* (London, 2005)

Wagner, Cosima, *Die Tagebücher, 1869–1883*, ed. and annotated Martin Gregor-Dellin and Dietrich Mack, 2 vols (Munich, 1976–7); trans. and introduction by Geoffrey Skelton, 2 vols (London, 1978–80)

Wagner, Richard, *Das braune Buch: Tagebuchaufzeichnungen, 1865–1882*, annotated by Joachim Bergfeld; trans. George Bird, *The Diary of Richard Wagner, 1865–1882: The Brown Book* (London, 1980)

——, *Mein Leben*, trans. Andrew Gray, ed. Mary Whittall as *My Life* (Cambridge, 1983)

——, *Werke, Schriften und Briefe*. CD ROM, ed. Sven Friedrich (Berlin, 2004)

Wagner, Wolfgang, *Acts: The Autobiography of Wolfgang Wagner*, trans. John Brownjohn (London, 1994)

Wapnewski, Peter, *Richard Wagner: Die Szene und ihr Meister* (Munich, 1978; 2nd edn, 1983)

Weiner, Marc A., *Richard Wagner and the Anti-Semitic Imagination* (Lincoln, NE, and London, 1995)

Westernhagen, Curt von, *Wagner* (Zürich, 1968; revd and enlarged 1978), trans. Mary Whittall, *Wagner: A Biography*, 2 vols (Cambridge, 1978)

Zemlinsky, Hartmut, *Richard Wagner: Ein deutsches Thema. Eine Dokumentation zur Wirkungsgeschichte Richard Wagners, 1876–1976* (Frankfurt am Main, 1976; revd edn Berlin, 1983)

Zuckermann, Elliot, *The First Hundred Years of Wagner's 'Tristan'* (New York, 1964)

Select Discography

Symphony in C major, *Faust* and *Rienzi* overtures, Bamberg Symphony
    Orchestra under Otto Gerdes (Deutsche Grammophon)
Das Liebesmahl der Apostel (and *Siegfried Idyll*), Pierre Boulez
    and Westminster Choir plus New York Philharmonic, 1978
    (CBS Records)
American Centennial March (Grosser Festmarsch), *Polonia Overture, Rule
    Britannia Overture, Imperial March* (Kaisermarsch), Hong Kong
    Philharmonic Orchestra under Varujan Kojian, 1983 (Hong Kong
    Records Co. Ltd)
Piano works on 2 LPS played by Martin Galling, 1963 (Turnabout records)
Sämtliche Lieder sung by Brigitte Sanady, Peter Maus and Klaus Lang,
    piano Etzel Grundlich, Kammerchor Ernst Senff, 1974 (Mixtur
    Schallplatten)
Die Feen, Das Liebesverbot, Rienzi. Recorded live in Munich in 1983 under
    Wolfgang Sawallisch and the chorus and orchestra of the Bayerischer
    Rundfunk (Orfeo)
Der fliegende Holländer, chorus and orchestra of the Bavarian State Opera,
    Munich (1944) under Clemens Kraus, with Hans Hotter and Viorica
    Ursuleac (Acanta, 1979)
——, recorded live in Bayreuth in 1955, conducted by Joseph Keilberth,
    with Hermann Uhde and Astrid Vornay (Decca)
Tannhäuser (Dresden version), recorded live in Bayreuth in 1962 and
    conducted by Wolfgang Sawallisch, with Wolfgang Windgassen,
    Anja Silja and Grace Bumbry (Philips)
——, (Paris version) Vienna State Opera chorus and Vienna Philharmonic
    conducted by George Solti (1971) with René Kollo and Christa Ludwig
    (Decca)

Lohengrin, live from Bayreuth in 1953, conducted by Joseph Keilberth with
Astrid Varnay, Wolfgang Windgassen and Hermann Uhde (Decca,
reissued on Naxos, Philips recorded it in 1962)
——, studio recording under Rudolf Kempe and the Vienna Philharmonic
and opera chorus, with Jess Thomas, Christa Ludwig, Elisabeth
Grümmer and Dietrich Fischer-Dieskau, 1964 (EMI)
Tristan und Isolde, studio recording (1952) under Wilhelm Furtwängler and
the Philharmonic orchestra and chorus of the Royal Opera House
with Ludwig Suthaus, Kirsten Flagstad, Blanche Thebom, Josef
Greindl and Dietrich Fischer-Dieskau (EMI)
——, live from Bayreuth (1952) under Herbert von Karajan with Martha
Mödl, Ramón Vinay and Hans Hotter (Orfeo)
——, studio recording of Barenboim and the Berlin Philharmonic with
Siegfried Jerusalem, Waltraud Meier and Matti Salminen (Teldec)
Die Meistersinger von Nürnberg, live recording from Covent Garden in 1997
under Bernard Haitink, with John Tomlinson and Thomas Allen with
the orchestra and chorus of the Royal Opera House
——, live from Bayreuth (1943) under Wilhelm Furtwängler (sound
restoration by Music and Arts)
——, chorus and orchestra of the Deutsche Oper, Berlin under Eugen
Jochum (1976) with Placido Domingo, Dietrich Fischer-Dieskau,
Catarina Ligendza and Christa Ludwig (Deutsche Grammophon)
Der Ring des Nibelungen live from Bayreuth in 1955 under Joseph Keilberth,
with Hans Hotter, Wolfgang Windgassen, Astrid Varnay/Martha
Mödl (Testament)
——, studio performance under Georg Solti and the Vienna Philharmonic
(1958–1967) with George London, Kirsten Flagstad, Claire Watson,
Set Svanholm, James King, Regine Crespin, Hans Hotter, Birgit
Nilsson, Wolfgang Windgassen, Gustav Neidlinger, Gottlob Frick,
Gwynneth Jones, Dietrich Fischer-Dieskau, Helen Watts (Decca)
——, Daniel Barenboim's Bayreuth cycle from the 1990s may also be
recommended (Teldec); early performances with Furtwängler from
La Scala, Milan, in 1990 (Music and Arts), also Rome, 1953 (EMI)
likewise, together with Reginald Goodall's London Coliseum Ring
in the 1970s (Chandos)
Parsifal, live recording of the 1951 Bayreuth Festival under Hans
Knappertsbusch with Martha Mödl as Kundry (Naxos). Re-recorded

in stereo in 1962 with Hans Hotter as Gurnemanz

——, The Royal Opera House's issue of a performance broadcast in 1971 conducted by Reginald Goodall with John Vickers and Amy Shuard (Kiri Te Kanawa appeared as one of the flower maidens)

——, The Berlin Philharmonic with the choir of the Deutsche Staatsoper under Daniel Barenboim (Teldec, 1991) with John Tomlinson, Siegfried Jerusalem and Waltraud Meier

Acknowledgements

The sheer mass of writing on Wagner necessarily means that any new contributor is indebted to a whole host of scholars who have helped, irritated or otherwise engaged him. My most substantial debt of gratitude goes to Dieter Borchmeyer, whose books and articles over the last thirty years and whose personal friendship have been a great source of encouragement, also to Hans Rudolf Vaget for many illuminating insights. Among British experts I must single out the work of John Deathridge, Barry Millington and Bryan Magee, who provided much food for thought. I am enormously indebted to my good friend Annette Zimmermann, who prepared the manuscript from my atrocious handwriting and helped me in innumerable ways to keep things on an even keel. But the greatest debt of all is to my dear wife, who has had the misfortune of sharing our marriage of nearly 50 years with a hectoring and intrusive ghost who does not like taking second place.

Photo Acknowledgements

The author and publishers wish to express their thanks to the following sources of illustrative material and/or permission to reproduce it. Locations of some works, not given in the captions for reasons of brevity, are also given below.

Photos by the author: pp. 131, 181, 187; photos © the Trustees of the British Museum, London (Department of Prints and Drawings): pp. 6, 65, 155, 175, 189, 200; from the *Illustrierte Zeitung* [Leipzig]: pp. 49 (7 October 1843), 95 (16 September 1876), 101 (23 September 1876), 108 (30 September 1876); from *Jugend: Münchner illustrierte Wochenschrift für Kunst und Leben*, issue 39, September 1900: p. 170; photos Library of Congress, Washington, DC (Prints and Photographs Division): pp. 67 (George Grantham Bain Collection), 147; Nationalarchiv der Richard-Wagner-Stiftung / Richard-Wagner-Gedenkstätte, Bayreuth: pp. 39, 182; private collections: pp. 103, 159; Stadtmuseum Bonn: p. 95.